ELSTEAD
THEN AND NOW

BY GILLIAN DREW

The Moat.

Published by the Author

ISBN 0 9541019 01

Printed in England by Arrow Press Ltd

CONTENTS

ILLUSTRATIONS

INTRODUCTION

The experience of a new Millennium, through which we have just passed, is something which has been given to few people in the course of human history. Now that the celebrations are over and the dust has settled, perhaps we can take a few quiet moments for reflection.

This is, if nothing else, a major landmark in the calendar of human history. It perhaps merits, for both people and communities, a look back at what they have been, an assessment of where they are and, building on these, plans for what they will be in the future. History, far from being "bunk" as Henry Ford famously declared, dictates, sometimes very strongly, that which governs our lives today. Far from being a retreat into the past, and an irrelevance, our origins have made our present, our traditions shape what we are now, and we cannot understand where we are, without an examination of how we got there.

This Millennium History of Elstead then is not a look backwards into the past for its own sake. It is the story of a living community which, although in recent years, in common with most villages, has suffered some heavy blows, is still strong and vibrant, still developing, and still looking forward with hope and confidence to the future.

This is a history of Elstead primarily for the people of Elstead, many of whom have contributed their recollections to it. It is a non-profit making exercise, and once the costs of production have been recovered all proceeds from sales will be distributed to local organisations. We will choose as wide a range as possible, so that Elstead in the past can benefit, even if only in a small way, as many as possible of the people of Elstead in the present.

CHAPTER I

BEGINNINGS

"Helstede", "Ellestede", "Elestede", "Elsted" and "Elstead" – the place has been called all these things, according to the changing fashion of the times, or, more likely, the eccentric spelling of medieval scribes, parish clerks and their like.

It is suggested that it comes from the old English "ellen-stede", "place of the elder trees" although no forms with the "n" are known, and the earliest mention of the name at all is in the foundation charter of Waverley Abbey in 1128.

Before the coming of man, Elstead during the Ice Age would not have been covered by the ice sheet which lay over the northern part of Britain. This area was an arctic tundra wasteland, with no trees, and plant species such as crowberry, dwarf birch and Jacob's Ladder now only found in high mountain areas of Britain. This information can be gleaned from analysis of the peat laid down between 10,500 and 6,000 years ago, in the Woolfords Lane area.

The loam of the Folkestone beds was, until the 1930s, largely under cultivation, whereas the sandy beds generally supported barren heath and woodland. The barren areas around Cutmill, Pot Common and Mousehill were thus characteristic of the sandy beds.

Although the name is not of ancient origin, Elstead itself has been occupied by man since the earliest days. The chief traces of his presence are the earthworks at Charles Hill and Britt Hill, northeast of the village. The Charles Hill earthworks were excavated in the middle of the last century and the excavators noted an embankment like a boundary line, running in a northerly direction, with five round barrows inside. These were opened but, disappointingly, without result. They had apparently been disturbed by earlier unrecorded excavators.

At Britt, or Britty Hill, the Rev. Charles Kerry, indefatigable antiquarian and local historian, Curate of the neighbouring village of Puttenham, discovered, also in the middle of the last century, some neolithic flakes, three arrow heads, and a spear head and a celt. So early man left some of his tools behind him; he buried his dead, presumably in the barrows on Charles Hill, but, beyond this, it is difficult to form a very clear picture of him.

"Poor, nasty, brutish and short" is probably an apt description of life in neolithic times. It would have been a hunting, foraging existence, the sandy scrubland of the area has never been particularly rich or fertile. It was not without its contact with the wider world, however, or possibly without its uplifting moments.

The chalk ridge, known as the Hog's Back, was a trackway of great importance, giving access to the entire west of the country – travellers would be passing along it as they would along the raised road that ran southwards from Seale to Hindhead, and commemorated by such names as "The Ridge" at Seale and "Ridgeway Farm" near Thursley.

The place name "Peperharow" two miles north east of Elstead seems to derive from "hearg" or temple, thus "Pipers Temple", and "Tuesley" and "Thursley" – "Thors Lea" in the area both have pagan religious significance. It is possible, of course, that it was precisely because communications were so good with easy access to major trackways, that the area became a religious centre.

"Thor's Stone", Thursley Common.

A hoard of axes was found on Hankley Common in 1911, which contained a palstave and two socketed south eastern type axes, one plain and one with wing decorations and pellets in the face. Both show signs of bad casting, and were presumably not finished for use.

The verb "hele" (or "heel" or "heal") still exists in dialect, and was in common use in the England of the sixteenth century. The meaning is "to hide or conceal, or to cover with a roof or thatch". "Helstede" could therefore have once been "the hidden place" or the "secret place", the centre of some religious mystery or the seat of an oracle.

The Rev. Charles Kerry, already referred to, thought that the name signified the stead, station or place, of Aella, probably the same Aella who founded the Kingdom of Sussex. This is obviously to a large extent speculation but Kerry did bring out two very interesting further points, in support of his idea.

There is another Elste(a)d, near Midhurst, which is even nearer Aella's territory, and the eastern boundary line of the Saxon hundred of Farnham, which was part of the kingdom of Wessex must have passed very near to, if not through, Elstead. Kerry sees it as quite natural, then, that the place marking the western limit of Aella's conquest should have been named after him.

The neighbouring village of Shackleford seems to derive its name from the ford through the "shakel" – a pond or pool for surface drainage. Elstead probably formed part of the ancient parish of Farnham with its Chapelries, in all 60 casati of land we are told, which were granted by the Saxon King Cadwalla in 688 to the Bishops of Winchester. In 909 King Edgar of Wessex gave the Bishops liberties over these lands and 10 casati more including the right to hold a hundred court, or local petty sessions as it might be described. This Charter is extremely important as it gives the first written record of the boundaries of Elstead, and Peperharow, although Elstead is not named as such.

"A erest act VII dican to Ottanforde, swa to Sumaeres Forda (Somerset Bridge) oouan to Ocanlea (Ockley Common) – that piece of boundary is the same to this day!

The village grew up near a ford across the River Wey, but on higher ground, above the flood plain. Elstead Green is 171 feet above sea level, and 50 feet above the river.

Saxon Surrey or "Suthrige" - the land of the southern men, was an area without many great centres of population, although the presence of a mint at Guildford argues a settlement of some significance there. We can imagine scattered agricultural settlements, most of the evidence for which now appears in place names – Britty Hill could be "Beorhta's slope or hillside".

We have already mentioned the possible origin of "Elstead" as "Place of the elder trees". Pudmore Farm could be "Puda's more" or damp land. Paulshott Farm suggests an Old English compound "pole-shed" or similar, from the Old English "pal" stake. Wychmoor Copse is possibly a compound of Old English "wice" – witch elm, and "mor" – marshy ground.

We have a picture, then, of a series of small settlements over the sparse heathland, interspersed with bog and damp marshy ground. "Fulbrook Farm" was in existence here in 1257. The name possibly comes from Foweles brok – fugol (a bird).

The River Wey had built up a rich but narrow alluvial river plain. At Elstead it was covered with meadows used for cattle grazing and when it flooded, between Elstead Bridge and Somerset Bridge the floods left deposits of silver white sand behind, six inches deep.

The boundaries of the parish have, of course, changed significantly over the years. It once extended as far as the Devil's Punch Bowl at Hindhead, and in 1905 the boundaries were Seale and Puttenham on the north, Farnham and Frensham on the west, Peperharow and Thursley on the east. The greater part of the parish has always been heath and scrubland, with habitation centred around the village green.

The River Wey crossed the northern part of the parish, and various clay depressions in the sandstone have filled with water to form ponds and bogs on the heathland areas.

In 1933 the parish boundaries were revised, so that about a third of the southern part of the parish, 1,354 acres, became part of Thursley. Most of this area was heath land, so it did not make a great deal of difference to the size of the population.

This, then, is Elstead, an area we can as yet trace only dimly. Let us move on in time, gradually picking up more detail as we go, until we find something approximating to the Elstead we know today, or, perhaps, that our fathers and grandfathers knew – "Yesterday in Elstead", in fact.

River Wey.

CHAPTER II

MEDIEVAL TIMES AND THE SIXTEENTH CENTURY

There is no mention of Elstead as such in that landmark in the history of so many other parishes, the greatest record of local government in medieval England, the "Domesday Book", or great census, compiled on the orders of William of Normandy in 1086-1087. William wanted a record of his conquered lands – it was of secondary importance when he sent his surveyors out throughout the kingdom what a magnificent record of who owned what, and of what value it was, he was providing for future historians. We know from the two Saxon charters, that the area was in the hand of the Bishops of Winchester, and this did not change after the Conquest. The Victoria County History thinks that of the six mills recorded in Domesday as having belonged to the Bishop in the area, one may have been Elstead and this would suggest that there was already perhaps a small settlement here.

The mills cannot be identified positively, but the site for a water mill needs to be fairly carefully chosen and, once chosen, is not easily subject to change. This, as Robo says in "Medieval Farnham" creates at least a strong supposition that the mill later known to be at Elstead was one of the same six recorded in Domesday Book. The mill is mentioned in the rent rolls of the Bishopric of Winchester in the thirteenth century: the water mill at "Helstede" had an annual rent of 10s.3d. in 1208. There was a new miller in this year, Osbert by name. In addition to his annual 10s.3d., Osbert paid a registration fee (purchasia) of 26s.8d. This was not heavy in comparison with some other local mills. There is no further mention of Elstead Mill in the Pipe Rolls of the Manor of Farnham for the thirteenth century, from which we may perhaps gather that everything went smoothly and miller succeeded miller in uninterrupted tranquillity, with rent paid regularly.

The first mention of Elstead by name comes in 1128 when the Bishop of Winchester, William Giffard, bestowed on the Cistercian monks from the Abbey of Aumone in Normandy, all the lands at Waverley with meadow and pasture, together with two acres of meadow at "Helestede", together with pannage, or grazing for their swine, and liberty to cut wood for fuel in his woods at Farnham.

The arrival of the monks at Waverley was to exert a profound influence over the surrounding area and one which lasted for another four hundred years. Not only would the Abbey have been the centre of religious life in the area, with brothers going out from it to build and serve in small churches or chapelries, of which Elstead was undoubtedly one, but the monks were also great sheep farmers. "England lived off the sheep's back", it has been said, with some justification, during most of the medieval period. The great sheep runs owned by the Waverley monks gave rise to the building of massive barns, to

Waverley Abbey.

store the fleeces, of which the one at Wanborough is a prime surviving example. Roads were needed, and bridges over the Wey, to move flocks and fleeces from place to place – the bridges at Eashing and Tilford still bear witness to this. Finally, of course, the cloth industry to spin and weave the wool into the woollen cloth for which England had an international reputation, arose at Guildford.

Elstead Church suggests by its architecture that it was one of the early chapelries of Farnham, begun around 1138, only ten years after the monks received their charter, and consisting of a chancel, a nave, and a low shingled belfry spire at the west-end, supported on very solid axe dressed oak timbers. Eric Parker, one of the most famous Surrey travellers of the twentieth century, enthused about the "wonderful ladder", up to the belfry in the church. It is, he said, "a single vast plank of oak, black and immovable, sloped up from a crossbeam, and notched for steps. There are magnificent beams in Surrey churches, but this is the finest ladder of them all".

Scratch dials were early forms of sun dial. They are basically found on church walls, and most in Surrey are late medieval, apart from the one at Stoke D'Abernon.

The scratch dial on Elstead church faces east rather than south, and can only really have worked in morning light. It lies at the bottom of the north jamb to the fifteenth century east window.

St James Church.

Frensham would seem to be the only other chapelry of Farnham with a comparably early date. Seale and Bentley were both later. Elstead and Tandridge are the oldest churches in the county to have wooden towers. By 1291, Seale and Elstead are recorded as being chapelries of Farnham, and we may imagine both churches being served by a monk from the Abbey for a few shepherds, swineherds and farm labourers.

We can gather something of at least two Elstead people of this period from their wills:

Alice Wheller.

13th August 1486.

To be buried in the churchyard of St. James of Elstead. To the mother church 2d. Residue to John my son.

Robert at Hole of Helsted.

10 Jan 1487-8.

To be buried in the churchyard of the Church or Chapel of St James, Helsted. To the Cathedral Church of St. Swithun Winchester, 4d. To the lights before the Cross and the Trinity in the said Chapel and to the light of St. Katherine, one sheep each. To the repair of the torches, one sheep. Residue to William Wheeler and Jean my wife, executors for the welfare of my soul.

7

Although the woollen industry declined in the area and, indeed, throughout the country from the sixteenth century onwards, it is interesting to note that the Victoria County History of Surrey, published in 1905, speaks of large flocks of sheep having been kept in the Elstead area "within living memory" – a throwback to the old days.

The Black Death was a form of bubonic plague which ravaged Europe from end to end between 1347 and 1351. Plague and pestilence were regular occurrences in medieval life. That this one received a special name shows that it must have stood out, certainly in the contemporary mind, as being particularly ferocious. It struck Surrey and one of the first victims in this area may well have been an Elstead man. William Waryn, was Reeve or Steward and managed the affairs of the hundred for the Bishop, but he died in October or November 1348. Maybe his family died with him because his little farm of one virgate went to his brother, Robert. His successor John Ronewyk, kept the manorial accounts which showed the devastation wrought by the disease in the area. From September 1348 to September 1349 the deaths of 185 heads of households are actually recorded in the manorial rolls. This, of course, takes no account of dependents. The average number of deaths of heads of households for the years preceding the Black Death was just over twelve annually.

Elstead is now beginning to assume an identity as a definite settlement. We find the name appearing in documents of the period – in the subsidy roll of 1334, for example,

Thundry Farm.

Elstead is assessed for £2.10s.6d. In the previous roll of 1332, there is a long list of individual assessments from the "Villata de Ellestede", among the more interesting being Petro ate Mulle, possibly Peter the Miller, with the highest individual assessment of 4s. Willelmo ate Sende was the only other individual with a 4s. assessment, and the top rate for the whole area was 6s., a rare assessment from a wealthy individual in Guildford.

In 1435, Elstead got a tax abatement of 5s. in common with many other parishes on account of "the depauperatorum" of the area. Why times were so difficult and the area impoverished it is difficult to say, perhaps there was a general relaxation of law and order as a result of the long minority of the King, Henry VI, and the preoccupation of the regency with campaigns in France.

Thundry Farm, at the junction of Cutmill and Farnham Road, was built at about this period. Polshot Farm dates from the fifteenth century and was owned by the Stovold family for 400 years, until they moved to Shackleford. The property has not been a working farm since the 1920s but constitutes probably one of the finest of the listed buildings in the village. In 1535, the Archdeacon of Surrey held Farnham Church, with the chapelries of Elstead, Seale, Frensham and Bentley. Although officially chapelries, both Elstead and Seale must have been parishes in some sense by 1539, as both have parish registers starting then. The first readable entry in the Elstead register says "Charity

Polshot Farm.

Mychenall was crystened in Elstead Church XXIIII die Martii Ano Mo ccccc tricesimo octavo (24th March 1538).

It is possible that the church was restored in the early part of the sixteenth century, as Manning and Bray, writing in the early years of the nineteenth century, say that the roof of the chancel was decorated with "a pelican in her piety". These were the arms of Bishop Fox (1501-1528) and it clearly is likely that the church was restored during his time – the more easterly of the north windows is of this date.

The church registers were sometimes used for recording other items of importance than births, marriages and deaths. In 1568, we read "Be ye knone that I, Rycharde Grover have fully parsed out of my yerse of prentyst wyth my father John Grover all thyngs payde and dyscharged the XV daye of August".

Although Elstead did not figure in the Domesday Book, it certainly must have felt the force of the next upheaval, which was to reach out and touch the lives of every man, woman and child in the land. The dissolution of the monasteries, and the granting of their lands to a new rich class – those who would support the King against the Catholic Church, who welcomed the breach with Rome and wanted a country estate to go with their often newly acquired wealth – this was the greatest social upheaval the country had seen for five hundred years. That very English of figures, the country squire or gentleman, strongly rooted in his native earth, tied in by self interest as well as conviction to the national church – this was the dawn of his age – and he often built a new house, or extended his existing one, to justify to the rest of the world how he was in the ascendant. In 1537, the lands which Waverley Abbey had held were granted to Sir William FitzWilliam. Elstead was probably passed on as part of the "site and possessions of the late dissolved abbey" to the Browne family. The Brownes held Waverley and "lands, tenements and appurtenances in Elstead". Other land in the area was held by various local landowners – in 1583, John Byrche conveyed two messuages in Elstead to Sir Thomas Bowyer, who held the manor of Frensham Beale.

From 1147 to 1536 Oxenford Grange was attached to Waverley Abbey. It may be that the Grange, as the name implies, was a centre of wool collection for the trade and in 1548 it was passed to Sir Anthony Browne, half-brother of the Earl of Southampton, who had received it at the dissolution in 1536. According to the Losely Manuscripts there was a house there occupied by Anthony Garnett, Secretary to Lord Montacute, son of Sir Anthony Browne. After Anthony Garnett, the house was leased by his nephew, Mr Lusshe, then by Mr Spencer, who was considered to be a Romanist, of doubtful loyalty. Certainly as the wool trade declined in the area so did Oxenford. On a map of 1594, Oxenford is marked with a church and Elstead Church is not marked. Similarly, in 1610 Oxenford is marked as larger than Elstead. By 1768, however, Elstead appears with its church, and there is no mention of Oxenford.

Litigation has possibly never been out of fashion, but it certainly flourished at this period. Disputes over property rights were, as ever, the most numerous and two of them in particular affected Elstead. In 1533, William Bromham and Alice his wife were in dispute with William Fillyp and Alice his wife, daughter and heir of William Westbroke. A messuage (house), 2 orchards, 40 acres of land, 10 acres of meadow, 2 acres of wood, 30 acres of heath and furze, 30 acres of moor and 8 acres of marsh were in question, making it a fairly substantial property.

There was a larger property at stake in 1555, when Lawrence Ellyott and Richard Strowde went to court about 2 messuages, a barn, a water mill, a garden, an orchard, 50 acres of land, 13 acres of meadow, 30 acres of pasture, 5 acres of wood, 30 acres of heath and furze and 6 acres of moor. It did not only lie in Elstead, however, but also in "Godalmyng, Puttenham, Shakelford and Chedingfold".

The new church had a somewhat stormy passage, lurching from one extreme to another before it settled into the safe, middle of the road, Protestant orthodoxy, which was the Elizabethan religious settlement. In 1547 under Henry's son the boy King Edward, extreme Protestantism was the order of the day. Henry VIII, in his own mind anyway, probably never entirely lost touch with the Catholic Church which had bred him and awarded him the title "Fidei Defensor" – defender of the faith.

He broke with the Papacy because it was politically and personally expedient to do so. It was otherwise with Edward, Duke of Somerset, whom he left as Lord Protector during the minority of his infant son. Somerset aligned England with the extreme Protestant faction in Europe, and set up Commissions to take inventories of goods, plate and jewels belonging to all the churches and chapels in the land They also turned their attention to abolishing chantry chapels, normally founded as a result of the wills of the devout, who left money to pay a priest to say masses for the repose of their souls, and those of their families. In 1553, by which time Somerset, after the uncertain fashion of those days, had fallen from power, another Commission turned its attention to church goods – to make more inventories to compare with the previous ones, and to enquire upon oath about property which might have been concealed or embezzled. Parishes were allowed to keep one chalice for use at Communion, and all other goods were to be sold.

The list of ornaments noted by the Commission at Elstead were:

I silver chalice

II Coopes, the one red sattyn of Briddgis, and the other a Sangwyne colored coope of sattyn of Briddgis very ollde.

I Sattyn Crosse

I Ollde Crosse of Grene Silke

I Aulter clothe of Lynnen

III Belles in the Steple waing bie Estimacon – the best iiiiC the second bell iiiC the third
bell iiC

II surplusis of lynnyn clothe.

All that lacketh of the former inventory were stollen by thieves when the Church was robbed, except 2 candlesticks which were sold for 5/- and the money used to repair the bridge.

Charles Kerry, writing in 1870, says that during the recent restoration, foundations of a wall were discovered, running across the nave, a little to the east of centre, as if the church had been extended at some earlier date. An alternative theory could be that the foundations indicate the front of the ancient rood-loft, which might have been constructed entirely within the nave, as in the church at Greywell, near Odiham. This idea is perhaps supported by the smallness of the chancel.

There were three bells in 1549, weighing respectively $2^{1}/_{2}$, 3 and 4 cwt. "by estimacion". There should have been three bells in 1865, when the new peal was made, at a cost of £46.16s.11d. but the churchwardens had sold the second bell, and a fragment of the tenor, to defray some church expenses.

There were no families above yeoman rank in Elstead in the sixteenth century we are told.

Muster Rolls record the stocks of arms available in each parish, and the numbers of men trained to use them in the case of national emergency. The parish of Elstead is not recorded as being in possession of any arms or weapons in 1569.

William Bronham and Richard Avenell were pykemen in Mr Weston's trained band of 1592. Henry Michinall was a Billman.

The muster of 1596 had 22 names, the others are all struck through. Tribes, Wheelers and Woodhatches are all prominent. Henry Mechemall is presumably Mitchenall, and Henry Wheler, Tayler, is presumably so called to distinguish him from another Henry Wheler on the list.

These men were not regular army members. There was no regular army in the sixteenth century. They stood ready to he called upon in case of need, and in times of emergency would collect their arms, usually stored in the parish church, and be available to fight if necessary.

The Elizabethan age was a great time for house building, extension and refurbishment. Even a yeoman farmer might add a wing to his modest hall house – something in keeping with the prosperous, confident spirit of the times. Several of the houses in the village date, at least in part, from this period. Brookside, in Cutmill Lane, has had an adventurous history. It started life in the sixteenth century, as a small cottage. It was known as Fullbrook Cottage during the early years of this century, when the Chillingworth family operated their hand laundry there, delivering the finished articles around the village in a pony and cart. The property was known as "Brookside by about 1959, when the actor, Peter Sellers, lived there. He it was who diverted the river to flow through the gardens. He was not to be the last famous owner of the property. Ringo Starr, of "Beatles" fame, lived there after him – an extraordinary development of what probably began life as a humble sixteenth century workman's cottage.

Two cottages in Milford Road also date from this period – "Berries", formerly "Peacehaven" and "April Cottage", formerly "Lilac Cottage", and previously the Post

Elstead Post Office and Jemima Blackman.

Office cottage. The two cottages together formed the Old Post Office and during the 1880s were the residence of Jemima Blackman, the village postmistress. The firm of Tracy's adapted "Peacehaven" to house the Telegraph Office, and the Post Office continued there, run first by Mrs Beatrice Martin, daughter of Jemima Blackman and her husband until it removed to the Green in 1952. Mrs Martin continued to live at "Peacehaven", until she died in 1957, with Bessie Blackman her sister. April Cottage was renovated and modernised by Tracy's in 1962.

Previous to the occupation by the Blackmans, the properties would appear to have been occupied in the mid-nineteenth century by "H. L. Bowler – Grocer". An old photograph shows his name board, with a double door on the right hand side, suitable in size for a cart. Once again, a sixteenth century cottage had a chequered later history.

Domford, in Thursley Road, was dated by the Domestic Buildings Research Group to 1550. It was a farm, and has a bread oven, a salt hole and a big open chimney. The owners held tenancy of the land under the Bishops of Winchester until the 1920s when one could buy land from the ecclesiastical commissioners. In 1795 George Legg lived in Domford, which was a farm and included a cottage now called "Little Barn" in Ash Lane. In 1800 George Legg, his son, inherited (1) pasture called Heathfield, lying at Staniford in the tithing of Elstead; (2) a parcel of land about 3 acres with cottage called Domford near commonfields called Kampsteate, in the tithing of Elstead – this seems to be near Pot Common; (3) plus a quarter of an acre "known as the same" with cottage now fenced around, and surrendered to James Legg – and his heirs. The later history of "Domford" will be continued in subsequent chapters.

Domford.

Peat Farm Cottage, in Red House Lane, is also sixteenth century in origin. It was once a farmhouse with a barn between it and Thursley Road, where the bungalow is now. It was built about 1570 and still has the bacon smoke place, a salt drawer, an inglenook and many original bricks and beams. It was still farmed in the early years of this century by a Jack Cooper, the owner being Col. Rushbrook, of Thursley.

Red House Farm and Barn began life in the sixteenth century, and has seventeenth century additions. Mr William Pierce, of Cock Hill, was born on the farm in 1903, when it was farmed by his maternal grandparents, Mr and Mrs May.

The "Old Farmhouse" in Farnham Road, had a sixteenth century origin, and a string of distinguished literary tenants in the early years of this century – among them being the widow of Joseph Conrad, the novelist, A.G. McDonnell, author of "England their England" and Vernon Bartlett, the war correspondent. It was a working farm previous to this, being kept by Mr and Mrs Chandler, the grandparents of the present owner of Chandler's Garage in the village. The small roadside cottage at the gateway appears to have had a somewhat bizarre use as a pickle factory in the 1930s. The actual pickle making was carried out in a barn at the rear of the property, and the product was sold under the name of "Cottage Garden Delights". It was also at one period the home of a cobbler, well travelled, from Norfolk, named Seeman. The Old Farmhouse is a hall house of high quality, with later additions, one of which includes an eaves cruck. Crucks, or large triangular shaped wooden braces, are common in some parts of the country, but very rare indeed in Surrey, and this is similar to the one at Littleton near Guildford.

Elstead Bridge is largely sixteenth century, but is thought to have medieval foundations. The importance of the bridge over the Wey to the monks of Waverley has already been mentioned. The original bridge is thought to have been built after the bad floods of 1233, in place of the ford, leaving a small ford on the village side. The brick parapets were added in 1826. There were probably more arches to the bridge at one time, as both banks have cutwaters and buttresses buried in them.

In 1565, the Bridge Commissioners reported: "Somersford (Somerset) Bridge is decayed and downe, and the cawsye thereunto adjoining, which bridge is the Queenes bridge, and

Elstead Bridge, 1930s.

by her highnes to be mayneteyned, the stones of which brydge were caryed away by James Bromefelde and by him employed upon his own buyldinges and Peper harowe upon the farm of Sir Richard Pexall Knight".

The present Mill House is sixteenth century in origin, but mention has already been made of Elstead Mill as probably being one of the unnamed mills mentioned in the Domesday Book, and as being worth an annual rental of 10s.3d., payable to the Bishop of Winchester, in 1208. Between 1231-1346, the Elstead Mill is mentioned fourteen times in the Bishop's Rent Rolls, and three times in the Farnham Court Rolls from 1574-1600.

In 1591, "the XIXth day of Aprell was taken up one at our mylle whose name was Toveth", the Church register tells us. It would be interesting to know who Toveth was, presumably a vagrant of some kind, and what was he doing at the mill?

In 1600, Robert Aston or Ashton, gent, held the mill, In 1624 Edward Beedle was miller. By 1647 when the mill burnt down, William Trible was the owner, and William Eldridge the tenant. Trible lived at Hambledon, so the Paynes who lived at Dyehouse on the Thursley Road, were responsible for paying the men at the mill.

William Eldridge was paid £15, quite a lot of money, on October 17th to buy a new millstone. The new mill was finished by October 30th.

What of the people of Elstead as the sixteenth century drew to a close? We know something about a few of them from their wills. John Wheeler a yeoman, or small farmer, lived at Westbrook. His will was proved in April 1599, and witnessed by Robert Aursell and John Stovall (Stovold), also yeomen. Annis Belade and Agnes Peniode were both widows, witness to the fact that women were by means despised in this "pre-women's lib" age, and that it was by no means uncommon for a wife to carry on her husband's business after his death, and to leave considerable property. Great interest can be gained from the executors of the wills, as well as the testators, in the first case it was Margaret Stovall, wife of John Stovall, in March 1597-8, and in the second, Henry Boxoull, yeomen, and John Lufe, yeoman of Frensham, in 1598. Some of these names are still in the area to this day.

There were a number of independent yeomen coming onto the scene now in most Surrey villages, possessed of a modest independence, and we can catch a flavour of them from their wills. Thus William Woodhatch of Elstead, yeoman, in 1599, was able to leave money to the poor of Elsted and Thursley, as well as bequests to a numerous family, and to his son Lawrence "the tenement in Thursley bought of Nicholas Kychyll and Alice Fawce".

Thomas Hoycke was interesting in that his occupation is mentioned. He was a bucket maker and leaves to his brother, John Hoycke, "all my timber stuff, my ware, both made

Saxton's map of Surrey, 1584, showing Elstead.

17

and unmade, and all my working tools." Once again, he made numerous family bequests and had a tenement, this time in Farncombe, to leave, as well as property in Elstead.

Gregorie Langforde of Elsteaad(!), husbandman, left, among other bequests, "a stall of bees" to his god-son Gregorie Boxall, in 1602.

William Chittie, a weaver, left in 1603, five children all under 21 and presumably a certain amount of financial uncertainty to his wife, Elizabeth.

Richard Gosden, who describes himself as a yeoman, is one of the few who mention a servant, Jane Decon, as one of his legatees. Another servant, Richard Ode, is one of the witnesses to the will.

In the Episcopal Visitations 1581 and 1582, the "Elstead Chapelry" had Edward Welshe as Curate. William Bicknoll, John Boxhall and John Collyn are mentioned as Churchwardens. John Collyn died in 1602 and his will is still extant, leaving his property to his son William and daughter Agnes Collyn, with his wife Jeane as executrix.

Edward Barton, Robert Aunsell and William Woodach (Woodhatch) are mentioned as parishioners.

In 1576, John Hampton was living in Elstead. He had a son William, baptized and buried there in that year. A few months afterwards, there is another entry in the register "the XXI day of January was baptysed the douter of Willaim Sporge, sayde to be the chyllde of John Hampton and named Amyss".

There seems to have been a slight problem in 1598 with intrusions on the Elstead Common Land from neighbouring parishes. Mr Vyne, of Shackleford, and John Billinghurst senior, of Puttenham, were both brought before the local magistrates, accused of driving their sheep onto Elstead Common, filching the common pasture from their neighbours.

3rd September 1601. The jury present "Mr William Vynes of Shackelforde for keeping of sheepe in oure common, and keeping of a staffered in oure common of Elstead, and so contynueth dailie, the Saboth daie only excepted, having no right there so far as we know. And further William Hampton, one of oure jury, doth affirme that John Billinghurst senr. of Puttenham, did saie that Mr. Beeden and Mistris Vyne of Shakelforde, did oftentymes drive theire sheepe to and fro from Shakelforde to a place called Bryttie Hill in the tithing of Elstede. But upon what rights he could not tell".

The infamous Vynes were no doubt people of some consequence, probably descended from the Ralph Vyne who purchased the manor of Poyle in Seale, in 1503. There are twelve entries of Vynes in Elstead registers between 1552 and 1690, the only Christian names being Richard, Thomas and Elizabeth.

William Hampton, the informing juryman was doubtless from the old-established family of Hampton in Seale. They also had a branch in Worplesdon, and one of their number certainly seems to have been active in Elstead.

The John Billinghurst who started this rumour probably came from Rodsall, between Cut Mill and Puttenham. The Billinghursts were certainly there in 1507, and still there a century later, in 1658, holding land from the then lord of Puttenham, William Leigh.

Hookley Cottage in Hookley Lane was a largely sixteenth-century building, which may have had earlier foundations, and was enlarged and modernised by Mr A.G. Collyer in 1914. Angus Taylor, carrot grower, was buried from here in 1600. Elstead already had its somewhat strange specialisation – it was well known for the growing of carrots! The Victoria County History of Surrey, written in 1905, mentions the great reputation the inhabitants had elsewhere for their knowledge of carrots, but says that carrot growing was not as common in the village as formerly.

CHAPTER III

THE SEVENTEENTH CENTURY

As England entered the new century there was a watershed as complete and final as anyone could wish for to make the beginning of the new era. In 1603, the old Queen Elizabeth died, after a reign of 45 years, as long as most people could remember. It had been the longest period of peace and stable government England had known for many years, although not without its alarms. The new Stuart dynasty was very much an unknown factor, and people awaited the new era and the new century. Bridges were causing some trouble in Elstead. There was also evidence, however, of growing organisation of local government to deal with local needs. A rent of 2s. per year was set aside for the repair of Somerset Bridge, over the Wey, on the road from Elstead to Shackleford. We begin to see a few more people coming onto the stage.

Elstead Bridge from a painting.

John Chesterton, who then owned Oxenford, died, and the estate was divided between his three daughters. Two shares were purchased by Sir John Platt of Westbrook, in Godalming and the other third held by Chesterton Fox of Godalming. John Platt finally sold his shares to Denzil, Lord Holles in 1676. When this spendthrift nobleman died, an Act of Parliament was passed authorising the sale of the estate to pay his debts, and in 1699 it was bought by Philip Froude, Esq.

20

The stable government of Elizabethan England was not to endure long into the new century. The first two Stuart Kings, although not without learning and culture, were to prove lamentably lacking in political acumen. "This I count the greatest glory of my reign" the old Queen Elizabeth told her Parliament, "that I have reigned with your loves". Her relations with her Parliaments were by no means always loving, but she knew just how to manage them to her best advantage. James I and his son Charles were not nearly so sure. Both were in urgent need of money, both were inclined to favour the cause of Spain in Europe and both had very little respect for the sensitive feelings of the thrusting, aggressive country squires and merchants who largely comprised the House of Commons and who would never vote the King money to support a Catholic power and, worse still, in the case of Charles I, a "Popish" wife.

Ship money was one of the more resented taxes imposed by Charles I and is commonly quoted in the school text books as being one of the causes of the boiling over of frustration and anger which led to the Civil War. Elstead was assessed for £13 in 1636 compared with Seale at £14.13s.4d., £13.2s.6d. in Peperharrow, £13 for Puttenham and for Thursley – an interesting sidelight on the relative size of these villages.

Flushed with the success of its victory over the Monarchy after some five years of conflict, Parliament was not without its own ideas for civil administration. Time was to prove that they lacked the machinery and perhaps the consensus to carry them out, but they started out in fine style, by dividing the counties into classes of a certain geographical extent, and nominating ministers and elders in each of the classes. These people were to preside ever the parochial election of elders, to certify the fitness of those named, and then to give place to the naturally formed classis of delegates from the parishes. On 16th February 1648, the "classical" scheme was sanctioned for Surrey. The first classis included Farnham, Elstead and Seale, but it is doubtful whether it ever existed in its entirety. The machinery, as has been said, was lacking, and there was also opposition from several quarters, particularly the Secretaries, a sect who were very strong in Surrey, and as much against Puritan discipline as anyone. There might also have been popular opposition, reacting against the excessive taxation imposed on the area by Parliament during the later years of the Civil War. The Churchwarden's Accounts show extraordinary expenses – on 5th May 1644, Elstead was assessed for four months taxes at £61.12s.4d. by the Parliamentary garrison at Farnham Castle. In 1645, 25th April, there was £14 for two months for the army of Sir Thomas Fairfax. Then there was £7s.10s. for six months for the "British Army"; by 1650, 28th September, this had become, interestingly, the "Scottish Army", with the abortive invasion by Charles II that year, and the calling of Scottish troops to English assistance. £8.6s.2d. was wanted for the "Malishra", In December, 1648, money was wanted for three months for the "Association" of English and Scottish troops. From May 1644 to January 1646, Elstead was paying £11 a month to military purposes. What effect, it may be asked, did this extremely high level of expenditure have on a small poor agricultural community? It was, obviously, considerable.

Several receipts for the Billeting of Troops in Elstead are preserved, particularly from the Paynes, at Dyehouse Farm:

"September the 4: 1647. Thes ar to certifi that I James Payne quartered Liftenant Evans and his man, and 2 horse 16 days, which were under the comand of Capt. Freemanne in Col.Ockley Reagment
Witness my hand
Jasper Evans"

"Thes are to sertify that quartered 3 horse and men 3 days at ffree quarter at James Paine having had 5 bushell of otes whoe belong to Capt. Ffreeman in Col. Okley Reagement.
F. Smyth, Henry Rayler"

James Paine seems to have been well and truly squeezed, but he was not averse to applying the screws himself as can be seen in this draft of a letter from him to Henry Martin, about non-payment of tithes.

"Mr. Martin, you are behind toe pay for your own Tyeth that you have detained unto your own custody for seven years past £24. 10. 8d. which I hope will make it good. I never had it and you are too pay halfe the charge of the reparacions of the Barne belonging to the parsonage which cost £7. 10. 3d. glassing of the chancell and all".

A number of questions leap at once to mind – where was the parsonage, and why should a "barn" have a glassed in "chancel" – was this some kind of chapel? Poor Henry Martin seems to have recovered from this burden of debt, anyway, as he was duly elected as Churchwarden in 1655.

In December 1648, £46.5s. of the money collected for the Association was refunded, on the grounds that the neighbourhood was exhausted by the previous quartering of the whole of Sir William Wallers' army. There must have been individual cases of severe hardship, and inevitably some popular opposition to military rule. 1647 must have been a year of some drama in the village as in that year the Mill burnt down. It may have had some connection with the quartering of troops in the area. In 1610 when Lawrence Eliot of Godalming sold the rent charge on the three mills to Richard Creswell of Badshot, for a payment of £50, and a yearly rent of £3, there had been a corn, a malt and a fulling mill at Elstead. The tenant was then John Shingleton. Evidence of the importance of the mills to the village is provided by the fact that they were rebuilt in one year, by the Stovolds, and the Chandlers, families still well known in the area. The cost of the new millstone was £9.15s.

The New Mill was "reared" by 30th October – of 1647 or 1648 – when workmen were paid 6s.2d. (31p) for beer. The "hedsill" was from Cosford and Robert Numan was paid 2s. (10p) for "grub-ing" it. The carter's beer money for bringing it to Elstead was also 2s. There is still a crater in the bank of the lane above Cosford Mill which could well be the place from which this very large oak was taken.

Elstead Mill, 1930s.

By 1674 John Price, "mealman", of Oking (Woking) was a tenant of the Mill.

"Ingleside" in Back Lane dates from the seventeenth century. It has been altered and possibly as much as trebled in size from the original. There is a local feeling that it was once a toll cottage.

Apple Tree Cottage in Thursley Road is listed as a seventeenth century cottage, but may have been built even earlier, around 1560. It was originally two back to back cottages, inhabited by the Ellis and the Butters families, but was altered to one in 1937.

It has a very large fireplace, a sunken dairy with cream niches, and a lath and plaster front covering the timber frame. The ironstone quoins outside remind us that Elstead was on the fringe of the iron producing area, of which Thursley was an important centre. Hammer ponds were connected with the iron works, streams being dammed to create water power for the furnace, and to run the wheel which worked a hammer for the smelted iron. However, after 1615 the use of timber as a fuel was prohibited because it was needed for ships. Coal was substituted for charcoal, and the iron industry moved to the sources of fuel and gradually withered away in Surrey.

The seventeenth century could well have marked a high point in the village's prosperity as a small agricultural unit, as a fair was held on the Green on St. James' Day. In 1666 there was a place called the "Dyehouse" out on the Thursley Road, the tenant being one Henry Peto. In fact, it was on the right hand side, descending the hill into Thursley from Elstead. It may be evidence of the cultivation of woad in the area. Guildford, Godalming and Farnham were all centres of the production of kersey woollen cloth, and the importance of the wool trade in medieval England has already been mentioned. The "Woolpack" and the "Golden Fleece" suggest the importance of the wool trade in the area, and as late as the nineteenth century, Elstead still had a worsted mill. The wool trade was dwindling in importance by the seventeenth century in the area, however, It was concern for the plight of elderly weavers which led Archbishop George Abbot to found the almshouses, or hospital, in his native Guildford.

There is reference in the Churchwarden's Accounts to a "parsonage house" in 1656, but there was certainly none by 1854, when the great ecclesiastical reorganisation of the parish took place. The field south of the Church was called the Vicarage Garden in the seventeenth century, and perhaps the cottage next door was the Parsonage house. Stacey's Farm, in Thursley Road, is substantially a seventeenth-century building. It was bought by Walter Ellis in 1919 from Cosford Estates, and run as a farm, supplying milk to the village. It was sold in 1936 to Tracy's, the builders, who altered it, and eventually Mr Jack Billmeir of Westbrook House, gave it to the British Legion for use as their Headquarters on 21st May, 1949.

Tumblers Cottage in Thursley Road, which is 17th and 18th century had a collection of names during this century. In 1937 there were two cottages called 1 and 2 Island Place, because a pool of water would appear after rain between them and the Church. The cottages were made into one and were apparently known as White Cottage in the 1940s. The name Tumblers Cottage had appeared before 1960.

Westbrook Farmhouse and Westbrook Farm Cottages date from the seventeenth century, or earlier. The farmhouse is now divided into two for employees of the Estate. The farm would probably have been the home of Matilda de Westbrook, who married Richard atte Rigway (Ridgeway) in 1654.

The Churchwardens Accounts of the period show Elstead folk taking interest in national affairs – there is a list of those who subscribed to the rebuilding of St Paul's Cathedral, after the Great Fire of London, in 1666. This seems to argue that Elstead, in the seventeenth century at least, could not have been quite the tiny settlement of poor agricultural workers it later became – there must have been at least a handful of more prosperous farmers. There is also evidence in the Churchwarden's Accounts of the very rough and ready social security arrangements of the period.

Ever since the dissolution of the monasteries, the poor had been a serious social problem. There were no longer regular hand-outs of food and clothes to the starving and out of work, and reports of bands of vagrants terrorising the countryside, and indeed the towns as well, are extremely common throughout the Elizabethan period. The Poor Law of 1601 was an attempt to remedy this social evil. The methods adopted were somewhat rough and ready perhaps, but they were to survive virtually unchanged until well into the nineteenth century, and in some respects until the coming of the Welfare State in 1945. Each parish was made responsible for the support of its own people who fell on hard times, Thus began the long era of parish officials diligently trying to shuffle off vagrants onto the books of neighbouring parishes. If the home parish was a long way away, vagrants were supplied with passports, by the overseers of the poor, to enable them to travel to their respective homes, which were bound to take them in. Large numbers of these passports were issued, and some survive for Elstead, which rather gives the lie to the commonly accepted idea of a largely static population in those days.

The Churchwarden's Accounts, which begin in 1591, give four notices of the punishment of vagrants in Elstead, and their provision with passports to travel to their respective homes. They were Thurstian Blackstone of Kingsley, Dorset; Joan, wife of John Brown, of Yarmouth; Edward Lanaway of Mebourn, Sussex; and Ralph Locke, of Epsom – the year being 1616-17.

William Bovington at work in the Forge.

Mrs Blackman the Postmistress.

The Forge, on the Green, is dated 1686. William Bovington is one blacksmith whose name we know. He had the Forge from 1870-1920, and lived in the adjoining house. He had been apprenticed to William Paine, and managed to buy the Forge from his master's wife, when Paine died. John Paine, who came from Tilford, had bought the forge in 1821 after he had worked there as a tenant for about twenty years. William Bovington was followed at the Forge by his son Guy, until 1952, when Guy Bovington opened the Post Office after Mrs Martin ceased to run it at "Peacehaven". The Forge was rented by A.J. Tracy and Sons until 1965, and afterwards by Mr Lucas and Mr Collis.

In 1662 a Hearth Tax, which as its name implies, was a tax on each hearth, was imposed to provide revenue for the Crown, in desperate need of funds after the Restoration, and the long years of Commonwealth rule. The tax was abolished by William and Mary in 1689 to gain popularity in the wake of their accession to the Throne. £69.9s. was collected in 1664 for 1,359 hearths in the hundred of Farnham. £94.17s. was collected for 1,877 hearths in the hundred of Godalming. The hearths in Elstead were 90 in all, of which 26 were deemed to be "not chargeable" because of the poverty of the inhabitants, in 1664. It was the responsibility of the parish constable to collect the money from the chargeable hearths. One, Henry Brookham, was landed with this thankless task in 1664 and in his list of names of those who paid we can once again find many families who are still prominent in the area – Richard Alexander, Edward Boxall, John Chandler, John Colyer, Thomas Crismas, Richard Denyer, Thomas Machweeke (this is probably Matchwick in Thursley and Madgwick in Puttenham), George Stovell, Widow Tickner.

CHAPTER IV

THE EIGHTEENTH CENTURY

The eighteenth century ushers in ideas of the Georgian era, an age of elegance in architecture, with Adam, Sheraton and Nash. When England had settled down after the early Jacobite uprisings, and the House of Hanover was firmly planted on the throne, there was a long period of peace, marred by the loss of the American colonies, and one or two foreign upheavals, it is true, but by and large an age of elegance, of luxury, of wit, learning and extravagance, of which the polished malicious lines of Alexander Pope's verse seem a perfect evocation. The artist of the era was undoubtedly Hogarth, who captured the luxury and extravagance but also the corruption and vice which often underlay it. This was also the age of church reform, and the amazing success of the preaching of John and Charles Wesley, aided by some savage attacks by many writers on the established church, owed much to the lax state many parishes were allowed to drift into, with livings held by absentee gentlemen vicars, many of whom never came near their parishes. The village at this time would have been composed of small field strips either of grass or ploughland, and a ribbon development of houses along Thursley Road as far as the Church, Milford Road and Farnham Road, with no connection between the three. As late as 1933 the field below the bridge, opposite the Mill, was still divided into seven strips, with the owners each cutting their own hay each year. This area must have escaped somehow when the Enclosure Act, which basically put an end to the medieval system of strip farming, was completed in Elstead in 1851.

In 1725, Martin Gruchy was Curate. He was also Curate of Seale – he probably needed to be in order to earn a living wage. He reported that the population of Elstead was about 300. Mr William Bishop, of Frensham, was lessee of the tithes, and therefore responsible for appointing curates. After the Reformation, Elstead became a perpetual Curacy, in the care of the Rector of Farnham, who would lease out the tithe revenue to any local magnate who was prepared to bid for it. Gruchy said that there was no dissenting chapel in Elstead, "no lecturer, no papist, and but two or three anabaptists of small account". There was no endowed school, and no charity, except "Mr. Smith's charity for poor persons not relieved by the parish". The "poor" still receive 25p vouchers at Christmas from the selfsame charity.

In 1713, Oxenford Grange was purchased by Alan Brodick, later Viscount Midleton. The third part which Chesterton Fox of Godalming had bought in 1624 had been sold to the Stillwells, of Mousehill, and this was bought from them together with the Mousehill Estate, in 1802. In 1775 most of the Grange was pulled down, except what was converted into a cottage, and is now covered with ivy.

The Woolpack Inn is reputed to be an ancient building. It was originally a farm and is rumoured to have been the scene of a murder. In 1758 the property was sold to the Goslin

Senex's map of Surrey 1729, showing Elstead.

family, who were wheelwrights, and it remained in their hands until 1843. The western end was used during this time as a butcher's shop.

Elstead House was a large, principally Georgian, house demolished by Hambledon Rural District Council in 1954. It stood in Milford Road and was surrounded by a wall from Ham Lane to beyond the present housing estate of Broomfield and Hazelwood. Two barns, one large and one small, stood between the corner of Ham Lane and the present flats called Barn Court and the Grange. The smaller barn burnt down and the other became a cafe, converted and run by a Mr Murrell. It was in use in 1963, but was pulled down when "The Grange" was built. The high stone wall ran from near the present entrance to "Broomfield". There was a door in it which led to greenhouses etc. then came the gardener's cottage – now the flower shop, and the hairdressers. The wall continued beyond this, with another gate leading to the big house, then double carriage doors opening onto the drive, with the barns and a shrubbery on the right. This drive passed the house and curved round to "the Park" where village events were often held. "The Park" extended in depth to where Ham Lane curves round, parallel with Milford Road to, and including, the present Hideaway House, in Ham Lane, and joined the present recreation ground, which was the property of Burford Lodge. Mr Charles Ingram, of the "Illustrated London News" and "Sphere" lived at Elstead House. He was a keen breeder of orchids, and his head gardener was Mr Bond. Mr Ingram was succeeded by Mr and Mrs Laddams, and then by a Captain and Mrs Reaveley. Mrs Reaveley sold the house to the Rural District Council on her husband's death, and they promptly demolished it.

In 1770, William Hogsflesh, the miller, took out fire insurance with the Sun Fire Office, as the fire mark fixed on the mill witnesses. Coverage was up to £200 until Michaelmas 1771, with a premium 4s. on his new dwellinghouse and brewhouse. There is another fire mark on the house of the Exchange House Fire Office, founded in 1708.

In 1724, it is recorded that Thomas Kelsey of Elstead, a miller, married Jane Flutter, of Guildford, at Puttenham. There seems little doubt that the mill functioned as a corn mill at least until 1777.

Thomas Kelsey, the miller, in 1724, afterwards opened a woollen mill at Godalming, which probably gave rise to the mistaken belief that Elstead Mill was a woollen mill. It is marked as such on the 1871 Ordnance Survey.

The lower rooms of the mill in the 1930s were said to be liable to flooding, and much damage had been done.

At least one person from Elstead was apprenticed as a framework knitter in the eighteenth century. This makes it reasonable to suppose others were engaged in textile related work.

Little Barn, in Ash Lane, was farmed from Domford by George Legg, a tenant of the

Rocque's map of Surrey 1765, showing Elstead.

Bishop of Winchester in 1795. He allowed his son James to have a quarter acre to build "a cottage with a paling fence around it". On the death of George Legg senior, the Bishop took his eldest son George Legg as tenant, of Domford, and confirmed James Legg as tenant of the quarter acre, now called "Little Barn", in 1800.

Tadmoor Cottage, out in Woolfords Lane, was built in 1765 – the name possibly meant "Toadmarsh". It was once a farm, and then became two labourers' cottages. It was converted to one private dwelling in the late 1940s.

Church Farm, in Westbrook Hill, was built around 1725 on land which belonged to the Church, and was administered, like the Church, by the Rectors of Farnham. It still exhibits a few bricked up windows – remnants of the eighteenth century window tax. There is an old story that there was once a tunnel passing from the Church to the farm and across the road to the old inn opposite, the Wheatsheaf, now pulled down but part of which is now Church Cottages.

CHAPTER V

THE NINETEENTH CENTURY

The 19th century saw the great upsurge in mechanisation and invention which led to England becoming "the workshop of the world". The invention of the steam engine, by James Watt, and the increasing use of coal to power machinery led to industrial concentration in the coal producing areas of the Midlands and the North. There was, generally speaking, a migration from the countryside to the towns with work available in the new mills and factories, although often under conditions of appalling hardship.

Very little of this would have been felt, at any rate to begin with, in a poor rural community like Elstead, far from any great manufacturing centre. In 1801 there were 79 inhabited houses occupied by 103 families. There were 225 males and 241 females. 274 were chiefly employed in agriculture and 45 in trade. The total population was 466. There was a steady increase in population up to the middle of the century as is shown by the ten-yearly census returns. In 1811, it was 521, in 1821 – 608, in 1831 – 711, in 1841 – 743 and in 1851 – 841. There was a slight falling away after this date, perhaps there was a drift to the towns in search of work. In 1871 the population was 756, in 1881 in was 679. There was then a steady rise to 775 in 1891, to 904 in 1901, to 1,036 in 1911, to 1,029 in 1921 and to 1,291 in 1931.

Truxford early Twentieth Century.

There was a pottery at Charles Hill until 1914. The clay was probably obtained from Moor Park, and the wood for firing the kilns was collected locally. The works were owned by one Absalom Harris. He later moved to Wrecclesham, where his son still had a pottery in 1937, and which is still operating.

The broomsquires with their wares.

The broomsquires or broom-makers lived at Truxford. The last real broomsquire was Tom Young who died before 1937. His son made a few brooms, but the handmade trade rapidly died out as it could not compete with the machine made product. The property was a wooden bungalow, and during the 1950s the then owner had an outside brick skin built around the building and the timber walls removed.

The area, as has been said, was agricultural, although some Bargate stone was quarried for building and road making. It is said that a "carrot bell" was rung when the carrots were ready for pulling. The coming of the railway in the middle years of the century was another great revolutionary force, akin to the dissolution of the monasteries, which was to have a profound effect on the entire country. For the first time, relatively cheap transport came within reach of all but the most remote areas. The full effects, as far as personal travel was concerned, would probably not be felt until the following century, when commuting to work in London became widespread.

It was perfectly possible to send produce by the new transport, however, and carrots were regularly loaded onto the train at Milford, to be sold at Covent Garden. At Royal Farm, Mr Ryle's farm, they grew hops, which were brewed in Farnham. In 1870, 32 per cent of the acreage of the parish was under hops and grass; there were 334 pigs, 297 sheep and

164 cattle – a total of 796 animals with 756 people! Wheat was the main crop, with barley, once again for the brewing, as a close second.

By 1889, communications with the outside world were becoming very good. There were two arrivals and two departures of post a day. In 1894 there was a circus on the green. It lasted two hours and must have been a welcome entertainment in a quiet rural area.

Maps of the Mill and Mill House dated 1841 and 1873 show that there was considerable building activity between these dates. In 1841 there was only a small house which was separated from the Mill, with another building shown to the south. By 1873, the house had been extended, and it then joined the Mill. Buildings had been erected against the southern end of the Mill, and along the river bank. The sluice gates associated with the present mill wheel are marked "Harris – Shalford – 1842" and it is probable that the wheel, which is of cast iron, and very accurately made, is also approximately of that date.

There is a popular belief, based largely on the Victoria County History, that Elstead Mill was used as a paper mill in the nineteenth century, but as Professor Alan Crocker has pointed out, this does not appear to be correct, as Elstead was not allocated a paper mill excise number for tax purposes, nor does it appear in the Paper Mills Directory.

The Appletons, who owned Elstead Mill from 1855 to 1881, certainly made paper and tissue at some of their other mills – at Sickle Mill, Haslemere, from 1860-1870 and their name is still associated with tapestry and crewel wool used for embroidery. They operated Elstead Mill as a worsted fringe factory, however, and closed it in 1881, as it didn't pay.

Mr John Baker, from stylistic and internal evidence, and by comparison with other local buildings, such as the Peperharow granary, deduced that the present mill building cannot possibly be the one which was built after the fire of 1647, and probably dates from around 1800. He felt it may well have been built to replace the corn mill, because although there is plenty of evidence to indicate the use of machinery inside, there is no evidence of there ever having been any milling mechanism – nor indeed is the construction of the floors strong enough to support its weight.

We are told that workers at the Mill, in the nineteenth century, sometimes had to get up at 4 a.m. to walk 10 miles to work. The Register of Electors for 1832 for the Parish of Elstead has twenty-five names on it. The undermentioned still have descendants of the same name living in Elstead and neighbourhood in 2001:

CHANDLER, George Elstead Bridge – copyhold house and land occupied by himself.
PIERCE, Irving John Elstead, Pot Common, freehold house and land occupied by himself.
REFFOLD, Henry – do –

Springfield Farm, had a large barn, demolished in 1963 (where there is a doctor's surgery,) and there was a hill behind it. Here, "on the platt" there was a spring in the corner which made a pond for watering cattle. Cows were driven daily to graze in the parkland behind River House and Elstead House, down the lane between River House and Tracy's yard. The house was owned by old Mr Job Ellis, after the death of Jim Collyer and then worked as a farm by others, up to approximately 1960.

Sylvan Cottage, formerly Ivy Cottage, was a hand laundry before the 1914-1918 war, owned by Mrs Denyer, nee Chandler.

There are three paintings from 1890 preserved in the "Woolpack" showing it much as it exists today, except the wing which is now the dining room was a humble lean-to, and the brewers were Lascelles Tickner. The premises had been taken over in 1843 by William Smeed, a common brewer of Godalming. They included a cottage, barn, orchard and one acre of land. There were several changes of ownership until in 1877 Agate, a Horsham corn merchant, purchased the "Woolpack". In 1891 the ownership changed hands again and the inventory included piggeries. The present dining room was once the clubroom where the village band practised, and the small room on the end had been a butcher's shop and a cycle repair shop, rented to Mr Bill Novell – finally, around 1924, it was the Co-op.

The Co-op at the Woolpack, c. 1925.

River House was bought by Sir Richard and Lady Jephson in 1870. They built walls around the property facing the Green. The property has been a farm and included extensive outbuildings. Charlotte Jephson died in 1913, aged 86. She was a great supporter of St James's Church and of the Band of Hope, a temperance society which met at the school every Wednesday.

Elstead Lodge, which is now divided, and known principally as Elstead House, was built in the early nineteenth century on land stretching down to Woodside Farm. At the back is a cottage, at one time used by the head gardener and later by a Miss Coomb, governess to the Chettle family. Stable buildings, etc, fronting the road on the west side were altered by Mr Chettle in 1977, and are now called Elstead Lodge. The big house was owned by General and Mrs Marsack for eight years from 1886 to 1894 during which time he was Churchwarden. They were followed by Mr and Mrs Pilgrim who gave land and money to build the old village hall, which carried a plaque to this effect. Mrs Holford, daughter of the Pilgrims, lived here with her husband in the 1930s. They were followed by Mr and Mrs. Chettle in the 1950s. Various parts of the grounds were sold off to build "West House" and "Freshfields" and the west and east sides of the big house also became separate residences.

The Hermitage was the home of Elstead's first resident parish priest, the Rev. William Jones, in 1829. It continued to house the priest until the status of Elstead was changed in

Elstead old Rectory, c. 1900.

1854 from a perpetual curacy, with a value of £4 a year, to a rectorship worth £264 plus a house, and the new rectory was built opposite the Church in 1862. In 1836 the Rev. John Hollier Stephenson was the incumbent of the "Hermitage" and in 1845 the Rev. Thomas Robert Docker, one of twelve children of John Docker, Rector of East Meon. He died and was buried in 1849, aged 46.

The next inhabitant of the "Hermitage" in 1849 was the Rev. John Ryland. In 1854 came the Rev. Joseph Charlesworth, first "Rector" of Elstead. As will be seen in a later chapter, there was a change in the status of the parish in this year. The Rev. Charlesworth continued to live at the Hermitage for another eight years until his new Rectory, opposite the Church, was ready for him to move in, in 1862. This was built on land "added to the Glebe by purchase through Queen Anne's Bounty".

Major Short, editor of the magazine "Broad Arrow", was the first lay occupant of the house after the Rev. Charlesworth and he was followed by Gen. Christopher Morris, who married in 1907, and died only seven years later, in 1914. He had extensive alterations made to the house. The "new" firm of A.J. Tracy was commissioned to pull it down, raise the foundations by one foot, because of flooding, and rebuild it again with the original materials. Mr and Mrs Spenceley and Mr and Mrs Gross are well known recent occupants of the house

Ham Farm and its stabling have been altered in modern times to form Ham Cottages. There never appears to have been a farmhouse there, although the land, which adjoined that of Elstead House in one direction and Burford Lodge in the other, has been worked by various people over the years. A Mr Hillyer grew carrots there, and sent two loads away to market each week. Mr Hardy stored the apples from his orchards in the stabling and Mr Dick May, of whom more later, garaged his carriers van there.

Burford Lodge was owned by Col. William Wolfran Gardner Cornwall, who was born at Elstead in 1840. He was educated at the Royal Naval School and Cheltenham College, and entered the Bengal Civil Service in 1861. He retired as a Magistrate and Collector in 1887. He married twice, and had May Cottages built in Milford Road, opposite the grounds of Elstead House. His father, Rear Admiral John Cornwall, also lived at Burford Lodge. He was Magistrate for Surrey and died in 1870.

There was a football pitch and a village school on the corner, on the land owned by Weyburn Bartel. Weyburn was first a laundry and then a garage for car repairs and in 1914 it became an engineering works.

The Bakery and Shop in Milford Road was owned and run by the Bedford Bowler family. Mrs Cheshire, nee Bowler, kept house in the adjoining cottage for Harry Bowler. His brother Bedford lived next door. The Karn family took over the bakery and shop in 1905.

Karn's Bakery, 1930s.

Avenue House, which was demolished in 1960, was built of brick-faced lath and plaster. The house was owned by the Terry family, and attached to it was a clothes shop kept by Mrs Sally Bowler, wife of Harry Bowler. Previously, Mr John Hurst, foreman of Elstead Mill, had the house.

The development of the Chapel, with house and hall attached, and graveyard and garden of rest in front, is chronicled in another chapter. It originally belonged to the Surrey Missionary Society in 1845. The British School was held in the schoolroom here until it moved to Thursley Road in 1847-50. Many pupils attended for half a day each week, and worked at the Mill for the rest. The two cottages which face inwards, towards the graveyard, were once four. They were owned by the Chapel, and rented out to tenants until 1868. They were sold by auction in that year at the "Golden Fleece", to Mr Stovold for £280.

The Star Inn was originally a cottage owned by Mr J. Hurst and used as a wheelwright's shop. It was sold to the Farnham United Breweries and the first licensee was Mr Martin Tidy in 1865. He was followed by Mr W. Trussler who had another role as a builder and undertaker, and stayed until 1922. Mr Ham, the next licensee had a small farm as well, up the slight rise where Springfield Estate is now. It must have been a daily sight – the men off to the fields at 6 a.m. calling at the Star with their half-gallon jars for the day's beer on their way. They had small horn glasses to use for the actual drinking.

In 1936 it was recorded that Hookley Lane ten years previously was a "mere cart track leading to one cottage. Now it is a tarred road, lined on either side with houses and bungalows". Eighty-nine houses had been built in the village in the last three years.

Hookley Lane was curbed and surfaced around 1970 but until the 1930s it was lined with apple orchards and the vegetable gardens of Burford Lodge stretched from the corner of Milford Road, down to where Silver Birches Way now is. The Orchard, now the second house on the right from the Springhill end, was the home of Mr Hardy senior, who owned the apple orchards, and the copse on both sides of the lane. Mr Hardy's son, Hubert, increased his acreage buying land from Col. Cornwall at Burford Lodge, and as has been mentioned, using the farm buildings at Ham Farm to store his apples. He became a builder, building a house for himself – "Dixie" – on Milford Road and "Old Bricks" and "Pegtiles" in Hookley Lane, so called because he built them out of reclaimed materials. Mr Hardy's daughter still lives in the village and a surprisingly large number of Elstead people still have very strong links with the area and its past, which perhaps contradicts the accepted notion of Surrey villages as being largely populated by commuters – "weekenders" who are bringing little to village life to replace the rich traditions of the past. There are, of course, many newcomers to Elstead, as we shall see in a later Chapter – there has been a great deal of house building in the twentieth century. The Chandlers, the Pearces, the Denyers and the Bowlers and their descendants continue to live in the area where they have been for many years, however. West Surrey as a whole has many examples of names which have been current for centuries – Chitty and Christmas are two which spring to mind. The result of this in Elstead makes for a great atmosphere of neighbourliness, of village community in the best sense, and this is something which will be mentioned again later.

The property now covered by Chandler's garage was originally called Sibley's Farm – the farmhouse being the area behind now known as the "Homestead". The whole area was owned by the Chandler family, who had a pony tub cart and brougham for hire for about twenty-five years, thus providing the earliest public transport in the village. They took people to and from Milford station. In about 1930 Chandler's had the village's first motor driven taxi, and the first petrol pumps around two years later.

Bridge House was a small shop, beer house and cottage when the licence to sell intoxicating liquors was transferred from the Wheatsheaf, opposite the Church, in 1860 It was transferred again in 1870 to the "Golden Fleece", next door.

The "Golden Fleece" had stabling and became a posting house for cross-country traffic. During slack periods the horses were used to haul lumber for pit props from the woods.

The Golden Fleece with horse and carriage outside.

For a short time, Bill Novell had a bicycle repair shop in an outbuilding before moving to a small shop in the end wing of the "Woolpack". He rented out bikes for the fairly modest sum of 1s.6d. a day.

The mill was closed in 1881 – Thomas Appleton being the last miller. The mill had been converted into a worsted fringe factory, making fringes for uniforms and dresses under the foremanship of John Hurst. William Baker was a woolmaker from Mountsorrel, Leicester, who came to Elstead by 1847 to work at Appleton's worsted and small ware mill, which made trimmings and braid for military uniforms. He married at Elstead but moved to Godalming between 1851 and 1861.

Fulbrook House was one of Lutyen's earliest works for Mrs. Streatfield, the mother of Mrs Violet Gordon. Her chauffeur, Mr Alan Collyer, father of Mr. Bob Collyer (previously of Hookley Cottage and then of Frensham), was the first man in Elstead to drive a steam car.

The group of cottages known as "The Square", situated where The Green and Thursley Road join, were originally six. Two, situated right on the corner of Hope Street and Thursley Road were pulled down in the late 1950s. The centre cottage, with the oak studded door, was a Dame's school, prior to 1898 when it and the rest of the cottages were bought by the Bowler family.

What is now Bargate House was the original Rectory, built, as we have seen, in 1862. The present Rectory was built in 1953, and the old Rectory became a convalescent home the following year.

Rose Cottage in Thursley Road was demolished in 1978 and four modern houses erected in its place. Mr Julius Caesar, the parish clerk, and his daughter, who moved to Liphook in the 1920's, lived there.

"Domford" continued in the hands of the Legg family and their connections throughout the century. John Legg, yeoman, inherited the property from his father, George, in 1847. In 1876 it passed to John's nephew, Jonathan Blackman, a farmer. By 1903 a Jonathan Blackman had become postmaster. He surrendered "Domford" to the Lords of the Manor of Farnham, and the tenancy was acquired for £700 by another George Legg, who was in business from 1903-1912 as a farmer and carrier on the Elstead to Farnham route.

In 1841-48, Pugin built a group of extravagant Gothic farm buildings at Oxenford, i.e. the Barn, Cowfold, the Gatehouse, Oxenford Bridge and the Chapel ruin, and rebuilt the rear of the farmhouse and its chimneys. In 1881, Henry Evershed Carter was made a tenant of Oxenford, taking over from William Chalcroft. He gave them up in 1886 and in 1887, 129 acres, woods 22 poles, were let to Mr Jonas Baker at £100 per annum, including Bagmoor Cottage. By 1896, he seems to have had 135 acres in Witley parish and 36 poles in Thursley parish. His descendants still live at Oxenford.

The original National School in Thursley Road, was built by Mr Harry Bowler on the site of the old tithe barn. An extra classroom was added in memory of Queen Victoria's Diamond Jubilee. The early history of the school is traced in another chapter.

"Cock Hill" is reputed to have got its name from the illicit cock fights which were held there. The area was largely owned by the Pearce or Pierce families and their relations. The Pierces appear to have given their children land at the back of their own houses on which to build homes when they got married. Thus, the houses backing onto the common without a frontage on the main road, are usually the newer ones. The Pierces were largely market gardeners and farmers. Moorside Cottages, Fairmile Cottage and Stanton Cottage, were built or owned by the family and their descendants, as were "St. Gorran" and "Wayside Cottage".

The White House, formerly Hill House, was inhabited around 1890 by Mr Alfred Allen, and his family. Mr Allen was Chairman of the Parish Council and owned property in Elstead, Thursley, Guildford and London. He had a group of terraced cottages built on Thursley Road, now opposite the school.

Where the road to Thursley becomes an "S" bend, alongside a bridle path, on the left, there is a white Ministry of Defence owned cottage. This was occupied in the late nineteenth century by a Henry Young, who made and sold birch brooms. Henry had two sons and one, Tom, went to live at "Broomsquires", in Thursley Road, after the gypsies had left their encampment there. The other, Harry, had a house at Hope Street, and both sons carried on the trade. Henry Young originally came from the Punchbowl, and collected his raw materials from the commons in the area. When Henry and his sons had a sufficient number of brooms for sale, they hired a lorry to hawk their wares as far afield as Cranleigh.

A parish room was built onto Church Farm in approximately 1850, for parish activities. It seems to have been built by individuals as the bricks are laid differently to the farm building. The kitchen was also added in Victorian times, so the well with its pump is now under the outer wall of the kitchen instead of being in its right place in the yard.

There was an Inn, called the "Wheatsheaf", opposite Church Farm. The licence, as we have seen, was transferred to Bridge House in about 1860.

Westbrook House was built by Thomas Stratford-Andrews for himself and his wife in 1820. The owner died in 1831 and is buried in the old cemetery. His widow moved to the Holt, in Seale Road, and the estate was bought in the 1850s by Sir Albert and Lady Levy. Sir Albert was a millionaire tobacco merchant. He built two pairs of houses for his staff and had a long lease of life at Westbrook. He was still there in 1935.

The life of the village changed considerably during the 19th Century. In 1889 the Working Men's Institute was opened. The Secretary was a Mr Morris, and the Institute was open each evening from 7-10 p.m. The village band was in existence by 1890, and the same year saw an early cricket match against Thursley. The School Boys Cricket Club started in August 1894, and was soon "going well". The band practised in the Club Room at the Woolpack, and the Recreation Society met in the National School. They organised cricket matches and possibly were responsible for the "new Coffee House, open all day" which sold "tea, coffee and cocoa at 1d. per cup, and soup, cake and buns at a halfpenny each, also paper, pen and ink", as recorded in the Parish Magazine of December 1891. Social life in an organised way was on the increase, perhaps to a large extent due to the improvement in transport and communications.

CHAPTER VI

THE SCHOOL

It has been mentioned that there was a school on the corner of the turning leading down to Weyburn; this was a Dame School, and seems to date from around 1837. The next school, The British School, was built by the Mill owner primarily for workers' children. It charged 2d. a week school fees and sometimes this sum would be docked from the parents wages.

The 19th Century, as it gathered pace and the speed of industrial development increased, provided many examples of individual self improvement and there was admiration of the ethic of self help as advocated by the Rev. Samuel Smiles and others. In 1849, Elstead's National School was opened by pioneering Church Men to serve the village as a voluntary Church of England School, to give the children elementary instruction in the 3-Rs.

Money was donated, and the school built on the site of an old Tithe Barn, but it was held to be important for the parents to contribute as well, and children in arrears were likely to be sent home for their "school pence". A Factory Act required apprentices to receive secular instruction in reading, writing and arithmetic for their first five years apprenticeship, and the children employed at Messrs Appleton's Mills continued to attend half time.

Plenty of fascinating information can be gleaned from the early log books. The numbers on the roll could rise to as many as 135, but attendance was often down to "a few scholars". Children from the Farnham Road area were often absent in winter because of flooding, or deep snow, and older children would often be absent for potato planting and picking, haymaking, harvesting, hop picking, whortle berry gathering at Hindhead, and even beating for local shooting parties. Further disruptions of routine were caused by illness – epidemics of diphtheria, typhoid, scarlet fever, whooping cough, measles and mumps. It was by no means unknown for children to die as a result of these.

Sometimes there was no fuel for heating – "temperature 32° recorded", and more than once the ink froze in the ink wells over night. In summer, the military manoeuvres in the neighbourhood caused problems between June and August and boys would often drop off to sleep in class through "having been out all night with the soldiers from Aldershot". There were habitual truants, requiring visits from the Attendance Officer, and many were absent on May Day, or on Clothing Club Feast Days carrying garlands from house to house. Sometimes there were so few attending that those who were in school were sent home again and it is small wonder that educational attainments were not high.

"The Soldiers from Aldershot", c.1880.

Masters in charge, perhaps discouraged by the unequal struggle, rarely stayed long, only one of them lasting the course for 10 years. They were supported, with varying degrees of success, by assistants, pupil teachers, monitors and local worthies. Many local ladies were mentioned for their assistance with repetition, sewing and knitting. The Rector, referred to as the "Reverend Gentleman" was a frequent visitor, teaching catechism and scripture – "Church catechism repeated by the whole School 3.30-4p.m.". It is noteworthy that inspectors frequently commended most highly the standard of religious knowledge in the school while deploring the writing and arithmetic, and the "tone of the reading". "Out of 26 present, only 5 got the following sum right in fifteen minutes – take 984,007 from 10,810,004".

Pupil teachers are often mentioned for poor discipline and presumably the master had to take harsh action to counteract this. "Reprimanded Charles S. for insulting pupil teacher, to be expelled next time".

There are frequent references to keeping the whole school in during play time and after school for being "noisy and disorderly", and "omitting to learn home lessons". Boys were caned for lying, impudence, truancy, stealing pears and fighting. Girls were cautioned for quarrelling, inattention, "fighting during leisure," and "dirty flesh". In 1877 "Bradford B. was punished for giddiness – not the first offence" and Henry B. for "taking William S's slate home".

In 1878, the Mill closed, and there were no more part-time apprentices as pupils. Average numbers improved, and so in general did performance. In 1893, however, things reached an all-time low. "The School is in a fearful neglected condition – not an exercise book for some time and no paper work except copy book writing. It has been necessary to suspend the timetables and substitute other work". In the same year, H.M. Inspectors found the school inefficient and threatened to withhold the small grant paid on results.

The 20th Century saw a much brighter picture of gradual educational advance. The Education Act of 1870 put the attack on illiteracy on a national basis. Board Schools were established and, in 1899, a National Board of Education. Since 1902, stage by stage, school life has been lengthened, a ladder built from primary education to university, new buildings and better equipment provided, and the training and qualification of teachers improved. The curriculum has broadened to include such things as science and P.E. As adjuncts to formal education, there are today school medical services, play centres, school meals, school broadcasting, etc.

Elstead School has progressed throughout this period. In 1917 the first three County Scholarships were gained, and today the path is clear from First School to College or University, for those who stay the course. In 1962, H.M. Inspectors reported that "these pupils are enjoying a full and rewarding school course". The buildings, however, were inadequate for increasing numbers (270 plus) and there was no hall or staff room and little storage space. Therefore, in 1969, a new school building, financed jointly by Church and State, was dedicated by Bishop Reindorp and in 1974 the school was reorganised under the Surrey Plan to become Elstead Church of England First School for children of 5-8 years.

The school today has an "Aided Status", which means that it retains the original Church interest and concern. A certain proportion of the Managers are Foundation Managers, appointed by the P.C.C. and the others represent the Parish and County Councils.

It is the early years, however, which retain the greatest interest, accustomed as we are to a situation where education is available as of right to every child, and where, even in times of cut back in educational spending, a full and varied curriculum is available. A further dip into the school log-books, before we leave the subject, would throw light not only on the condition of the school 100 years ago, but also give some insight into the lives of the children and their parents.

1864 – October 6th
School noisy and disorderly during first part of morning; kept in during play time for the same. First and Second classes kept back for omitting to learn home lessons.

1864 – December 10th
Several (10) children absent on account of Clothing Club.

1867 – August 9th
Several children absent this week on account of their being employed on gathering the harvest.

1868 – January 20th
Six boys were punished for smoking.

1868 – March 3rd
A gentleman called and gave the children some sound advice.

1868 – May 1st
Thin attendance – children absent carrying May garlands from house to house

1868 – September 1st
Work resumed after usual hop picking vacation of one month.

1869 – December 6th
Emily aged 12 admitted, being unable to read her letters.

1871 – January 17th
Attendance thin, the road to the Mill being impassable through water.

1874 – June 22nd
Very large attendance (135).

1875 – March 5th
Sent Thomas C. home. He was taken ill with violent retching through poison. Died in the evening,

1875 – March 22nd
Sent William W. home for his school fees – 8 weeks in arrears.

1880 – November 8th
Children cautioned on account of coming to school with dirty flesh and dirty heads.

1889 – August 4th
Alfred Hockley, aged 8 years, died from burns. Unexploded cartridges in his pocket were ignited by a heath fire and although he tried to put it out with water from a small stream he was badly burned. He died in hospital.

1893 – May 25th
H.M.I's report quotes elementary attainments much below par. School inefficient – grant therefore may be withheld. Premises must be properly cleaned. This was the worst report ever.

1894 – August-September
Schoolboys Cricket Club started out of school hours and going well.

1894 – October 26th
Numbers on books 94 – average attendance 58.

1901 – February 14th
Temperature was 36°. Impossible for the children to work "creditably".

1901 – February 15th
A 'chaldron" of coke brought by Mr. Legg.

1901 – November 25th
Children began to take drill on Wednesdays from 3-3.30p.m.

1902 – June 26th
Holiday for Intercessions for King Edward VII. School opened as usual due to postponement of Coronation.

1902 – December 11th
Children present at planting of Coronation Tree on Green.

1905 – May 24th
Holiday – Empire Day. H.M. The King in the neighbourhood. Children marched in the playground and saluted the flag.

1905 – August
School closed – epidemic of scarlet fever. In this year the doctor began examining all children of all age groups.

1912 – January 22nd
An epidemic of influenza – the first mention of the disease by name. It occurred every year after this.

1913
H.M.I.'s report "premises have much improved".

1915 – February 25th / April 12th
School used by Military Authorities for soldiers quarters.

1916 – September 20th
New subjects have been introduced:- Drawing, Woodwork and Household Management. School Playing Fields taken for allotments.

1917 – August 3rd
Junior County Scholarships, the first ever gained.

1932 – August 29th
Attendance Officer visits regularly – attendance much better, 174 on the books.

1935
H.M.I's report – number on roll 151. Parents engaged in agriculture, broom making and engineering.

1939 – September 14th
School re-opened, 167 on roll. There were a number of air raid warnings and some of the children took shelter in trenches dug by the Church. An old hut, previously used for chickens, was erected in the playground to become the school canteen.

There were air raid warnings nearly every day in September 1940. In 1941 the National Savings Group was started, and on June 28th 1944, a day which must have lived long in the memory of all the inhabitants of the village, there were five alerts, and two rocket bombs passed over Elstead.

This sees the end of the early log books which make fascinating reading, as they chronicle not only the early years of struggle as a small country school in a poor area gradually improves its standards, but also provide a graphic record of the social history of the time as national events intrude into village life and we read of the illnesses, the holidays, the occupations, and even the economic background of the children and their parents.

CHAPTER VII

RELIGIOUS LIFE

There were significant changes in the religious life of the village during the 19th century. There has already been mention made of the change of status at St James. By 1811, Frensham, Seale and Elstead had been separated from Farnham for civil purposes, but they were still linked for ecclesiastical. The tithes of Farnham and its dependent chapelries were habitually let out by the archdeacons for a term of three lives, with fines on renewal, and the right of nomination of a curate. In 1840, Bishop Sumner introduced a Bill in the Lords to anticipate the calling in of the leases, and to restore the tithe money to the parishes, but it was opposed and withdrawn.

There was a period of controversy between Archdeacon Utterton of Farnham and several interested laymen concerning the application of the tithes to the endowment of the parishes. An Order in Council was finally made on the 29th November 1865, by which the tithe rent charges in Frensham, Seale, Elstead and Bentley, formerly held by the Archdeaconry of Surrey, were given over to endow the several Churches as the leases by which they had been rented out fell in.

There were some additions to the church, as if to celebrate the new status of the parish. In 1871-72 a vestry and organ chamber were added on the south side of the chancel and

Elstead Church by Petrie, between 1780 and 1808.

a south aisle and south porch were built. New seating was installed and a new pulpit, carved by a Miss Cornwall. The new organ was installed in 1875 by a Birmingham firm of organ builders at a cost of £180. The font had a somewhat chequered history during the course of the 19th Century. In 1811, Manning and Bray described the font in the church as being cylindrical and of sandstone. This mysteriously disappeared. Bishop Sumner gave the church a new font in 1845, but before that the Rev. J.R. Charlesworth, Rector from 1854 to 1904, had heard that children were baptised from a china basin on the communion table.

The Rev. Charlesworth, who was obviously a notable figure in village life in the 19th Century, is recorded as a frequent visitor to the fledgling school. He was of the opinion that the barrel-shaped sandstone font at St Martha's was the same one which Manning and Bray had described as being in Elstead Church. It was very similar to the one in Thursley Church, which perhaps would support this idea. Born in 1821, the Rev. J.R. Charlesworth was 33 when he first came to Elstead. He died 27th September 1904, aged 83, after working in Elstead for 50 years and is buried in the churchyard.

There is an interesting insight into church life in Elstead immediately before he arrived contained in notes made in front of the Burial Register for 1849 by John Ryland, the last "perpetual curate" appointment.

In November 1849 the Churchyard was planted with limes and a cedar tree, from the proceeds of the collection taken at the Service of Thanksgiving for the removal of the cholera epidemic.

On November 27th 1849, the Church Green was planted, through the kindness of John Cornwall junior. Three days later, the pathway was curbed and posts were erected along Church Lane.

In October 1850, two lamps were obtained for the church by subscription. In 1851 the hole at the east end of the school was filled up and two yews were planted in the churchyard in November.

In 1852, the year began with the presentation of a lending library of 57 volumes by W. Ewart M.P. Also the hole on the west side of the school house – which seems to have been surrounded by holes! – was filled in with 250 loads of earth. This year also saw the beginning of the public subscription for the organ which was eventually installed in 1875. In 1853 there was "a walk around the churchyard to the school gates", for what purpose it is not quite clear.

The churchyard was enclosed by a paling fence with different farms responsible for their own portion or "panel" to keep it in good repair. "Owners" of the fence on the north side had made a stone wall for their portion, and in 1863, the other "owners" agreed to do the same. In February 1865, the Bishop of Winchester consecrated some "waste land" taken into the cemetery as the pressures on the churchyard were fairly constant. In July 1894, as space was getting short once again, it was decided to purchase more ground. Enquiries were made about the possibility of purchasing from Col. Rushbrook "an acre of land in the field near the road on the side of the path opposite the school's shrubbery and playground".

In a drawing of the church of approximately 1820 viewed from the north, there are no trees around the boundaries of the churchyard. There are 12 graves of Stovolds near the churchyard wall, and numerous graves of the Legg family.

About the year 1819, the Surrey Mission had introduced the preaching of the Gospel in their style to Elstead. A congregation of Protestant dissenters was formed, and in 1834, they organised into a church of 15 members with the Rev. Hillyard as Pastor. The congregation was chiefly made up of farm labourers, and those in humble circumstances. From 1834-1845 worship was conducted in a room hired from the British School. On September 9th 1845 the Little Napson estate was bought from Mr Joseph Sturdy for £550. The money was lent by Mrs Sarah Legg, and the property was surrendered to her in the first instance with a view to a mortgage. Mrs Legg was a widow, of Peperharow, and she lent the £550 at 4 per cent per annum. The property consisted of:

Elstead Church 1862, by W. F. Saunders.

1. a small parcel of land called Little Napson of half an acre with appurtenances;
2. the east end of the garden adjoining the dwelling house, late of Nathaniel Marchant;
3. one parcel of land, late of waste soil enclosed in front of the dwelling house late of the Rev. George West.

The Rev. S. Hillyard "closed his labours here" on February 23rd 1840 and was succeeded by the Rev. John Moss. The numbers in the church had by this time risen to 41 and in 1837, a Wormley Branch of the Congregational Church had been formed, with five members transferred from Godalming.

Mr Dixon of Godalming was the architect for the new chapel building, and on May 9th 1845 the contract for £395 was given to Hills of Arundel.

The foundation stone was laid on June 3rd 1845 by Mrs Legg of Royal Farm. The scene was graphically described by the local paper – "An immense tent was erected on the site which was most tastefully decorated by some of the young ladies of the village with scriptural devices and ornamental flower work. After the ceremony nearly 300 persons sat down to tea, which, being concluded, the meeting was addressed by several of the neighbouring ministers. Our beautiful village presented a most animated appearance, and, the day being remarkably fine, the whole passed off most pleasantly."

A copy of the document of dedication read at the foundation service was put in a bottle under the foundation stone, together with a silver shilling, sixpence and fourpenny piece of the reign of Queen Victoria and a halfpenny of George III.

The new chapel was erected on a piece of waste land, but the estate as purchased from Joseph Sturdy contained properties already. Firstly there was the house and premises occupied by the Rev. Edward Bromfield who had by this time succeeded the Rev. Moss as Minister. Secondly, there were four cottages, occupied by James Chitty, William Reffold, Robert Heath, and Luke Heath respectively. Lastly there was the school room adjoining the dwelling house of the Rev. Bromfield which was used as a place of worship prior to the building of the chapel, and also a British Day School and Sunday School.

The new chapel was opened for public worship on April 10th 1846. Pew seats were charged at the rate of 1s. or 6d. per sitting per quarter. Friends of the Sabbath School purchased alphabets by which to instruct the little ones in the "Look and Say" system. These were shown to church members and applauded.

In 1857 a church opened at Tilford. To avoid a clash of times, services at Elstead and Tilford were on alternate Sabbath mornings and afternoons.

On August 1st 1859, the Rev. Bromfield died, and the following year, the Rev. A. Heal was called to the Elstead Ministry. The Surrey Mission paid him £90 a year and the church at Elstead was responsible for the rent and taxes on his house.

On the 1st December 1865, a Miss Robinson of Guildford, and many from the army at Aldershot came to Elstead and held a Temperance Service. Of the 400 present 40 signed the pledge, and a Temperance Society was formed in the village. It had a band and initially 45 members. The Band of Hope met in the School Room every Wednesday.

In 1866 a new Minister, Mr Simeon Leete, took over. The state of the church was very discouraging, with much division and poorly attended services. By the following year, things had improved slightly and weekly offerings were now started instead of pew rents, which improved the financial situation.

By 1867 the debt on the purchase of the estate and the building of the chapel totalled £800, on which interest was being charged at the rate of £36 per annum. It was decided that the church could not carry on with this debt, and the support of the Minister. A praiseworthy resolve was made to extinguish the debt by the end of the year. Various means of doing this were calculated. The common land belonging to the estate was sold to a Mr Trismer in 1868. The four cottages were sold by auction at the "Golden Fleece" to Mr Stovell. This raised a total of £430. £120 was raised from among the congregation themselves. Mr Appleton promised to contribute £50 if the congregation gave £50. £250 was raised by appeal to wealthy Christian friends in the county and elsewhere. It was announced that "cheques and postal orders on Godalming or stamps will be received by Thomas G. Appleton, Esq., of Elstead, Treasurer of the Fund".

Finally, there was the Bazaar. This was no ordinary bazaar. It lasted three days, and raised a total of £94.19s.7d. It was advertised widely as "a Bazaar in aid of the extinction of the debt upon the Chapel", and "the assistance of kind Christian friends" was "earnestly requested" for "contributions of articles of utility, such as used clothing etc. suitable for an agricultural population, as well as those of an ornamental kind". Mrs and Miss Appleton of Elstead Mills were the appointed recipients of all donations, and by Good Friday 1869, the 24th anniversary of the church, a special service was held to celebrate the extinction of the debt.

An examination of the names of subscribers to the chapel, and church members of the period, together with names on the graves in the burial ground, yields many of the well-known families in the village both then and since. The Appleton family, owners of the Mill, were prominent church supporters. The infant son of Jesse Blackman was buried on February 16th 1850. In 1858, on November 16th, Moses Swansbury, aged 2 years, son of George Swansbury, commonly called George Larke, was buried in the same grave as James Luke. These, we are told, were "very poor people" and no charge was made. The Budds, the Caesars, the Chittys and the Larbys all figure in the records.

The high point of 1869, with the debt paid off, and all "set fair" was not to last, however, In December 1871, the Surrey Mission Society decided that they could not continue to employ Pastor Leete, and as the church could not support him, he resigned in August of the following year. The last services were held in the chapel on October 6th 1872.

Cleal in "Congregationalism in Surrey", suggests that the difficulties of the church were increased "by the removal of a local industry", i.e. the worsted mill, which finally closed in 1881. This is extremely plausible, especially when one considers that the Appleton family, the mill owners, were among the staunchest pillars of the church. Their loss must have been a sad blow to a small community. The agricultural depression of the 1870s and resulting poverty among farm labourers may have been another contributing factor.

The church did not close entirely. For some time it was under the oversight of the Church of Farnham. Around 1890, the Congregational Church at Godalming, took over responsibility and Elstead gained strength again as an out-station of this church.

One regular attender at the chapel during this period had been something of an infant prodigy! By 1881, Miss Nelly Wateridge and her father had settled in Elstead. Nelly, aged 15, had toured halls between Petersfield and Southampton, giving two-hour long recitations. "The Prodigal Son" and "Closing Scenes of the Life of Christ", accompanied by her father, operating a "very powerful phantasmagoria lantern" using "oxy-calcium light" to project hand painted lantern slides. Nelly lectured at the "Independent Chapel" as the church was then called and accompanied the choir on the harmonium while her father manipulated the triplexion lantern! The following Christmas, 1883, saw her reciting the "Story of Jane Conquest" at the prize-giving of St James Church Sunday School, and in the same year, she gave an "interesting lecture" accompanied by "dissolving slides" at Milford. She eventually married a Mr Chalcroft who in partnership with Mr Bovington, ran the smithy on the Green. The descendants of the redoubtable Nelly still live in the village.

CHAPTER VIII

TWENTIETH CENTURY – PEOPLE AND PLACES

The 20th Century heralded an era of tremendous change in every walk of life. Technological advance ushered in an age of enormous mobility – social and geographical. Not only did people improve their own prospects in life through improved educational opportunities, but for the first time it became common place to think of living and working anywhere in the country or, indeed, the world.

The effect of all this on small country villages, especially those close to the great magnet of London, is not difficult to imagine. A book published a few years ago was entitled "The End of Tradition – Country Life in Central Surrey". It is fashionable to lament the passing of traditional rural life, and the invasion of what were once the homes of local people by "week-enders", working in the towns, and contributing little to the life of the village community. The passing of the old country crafts was lamented as long ago as 1880 by Gertrude Jekyll, artist, photographer and landscape gardener extraordinary in her hook "Old West Surrey"

Although there has been a revival of rural crafts in recent years, it is true to say that they have largely died out in the face of competition from the mass-produced product. It is with the people that we see the least change. Although Elstead has seen a tremendous influx of population with much new building, Elstead people have always been firmly rooted in their native heath, given to moving around the village perhaps, in their progression through life, from a big house to a small one, but never leaving the village entirely. We have already remarked on the continuity of families in the area, and this has continued to be the case all through the changes of two world wars, and countless other upheavals. Even today, a significant proportion of the population have parents and even grandparents from the village and, whether as a result of this or not, it is hard to say, community life flourishes.

Transport and communication are one of the main areas where village life has seen most changes in the present century. The coming of motorised transport, and its spreading throughout all sections of the population so that nowadays it is an unusual family without a car, not only encourages travel, it brings national and international affairs into the life of the village, and manufactured goods and foodstuffs too, in a way that would have been unthinkable a century ago. The first telephone was installed in 1913 and by 1936 there were "well over 100 telephones in the village".

There is a very interesting study of Elstead compiled in 1936 by Olive Medcalf as part of her teacher training course, and now itself of considerable historic interest. She said that very few of the older inhabitants had single occupations – the Farnham carrier was the Sexton, the farmer ran a milk round etc. Bakers delivered in the village from Godalming

OCTOBER, 1909.

Canterbury

ST. JAMES', ELSTEAD,
Parish Magazine.

Rector: REV. R. M. CURWEN, M.A.

CHURCH COUNCIL.
Churchwardens:
Messrs. G. STREATFEILD and C. MORRIS.

Sidesmen:
Messrs. G. COOPER, M. EDWARDS, H. E. ETHERINGTON, H. O. HOLFORD,
G. LEGG, C. LAWRENCE, M. PEARCE, and J. RALPH.

Organist:
Mr. E. W. PILLINGER

Choir Representatives:
Messrs. A. BONNER, H. L. BOWLER, G. COLLYER, and H. ELLIS.

SERVICES.

SUNDAY. Holy Communion. 1st Sunday in the Month, 8 a.m.
and at Mid-day; 2nd, 4th, and 5th Sundays
8 a.m.; 3rd Sunday, after Mattins, 12 noon.

Mattins, every Sunday, 11 a.m.

Children's Service, every Sunday, 3 p.m.

Evensong, every Sunday, 6.30 p.m.

Litany, 1st and 3rd Sundays, 2.45 p.m.; 2nd and 4th
Sundays, at Mattins; 5th Sunday, at Evensong.

Holy Baptism, any Sunday, 3.45 p.m.

SAINTS' DAYS. Holy Communion, 8 a.m. (if desired).

Mattins, 11 a.m.

Notices of Baptisms, Churchings, Marriages, or Burials to be
given to MR. C. FITKEN, Sexton.

MORAY, ROSS & CAITHNESS.

ST. DAVIDS.

PRICE ONE PENNY.

Parish Magazine, 1909.

George Legg's Carrier Cart.

and even Grayshott in those supposedly less civilised days, so local people had a good choice of tradesmen.

Mr George Legg and his carriers cart have already been mentioned. This would have been the only public vehicle at the turn of the century. It plied to Godalming and back daily, and to Guildford twice a week, on Tuesday and Friday. Chandlers have been mentioned as having their pony and trap for hire and these two represented public transport in Elstead up until the First World War.

In 1914, Mr E. Medcalf bought the carriers business from Mr Legg, and after the war Mr Dick May, one of the great figures in the modern life of the village, started his carriers round.

May's Motors was founded in 1920. He began as a general carrier, with a small van, "buying out" the round of another man. His route ran from Cock Hill to Shackleford, Hurtmore, and Charterhouse to Godalming and back to Elstead over the same route. Cards with a large "M" in house windows showed him that his services were needed, at 3d. per parcel. Helped by his brother, he then started in the haulage business, and then a bus company. Mays made four trips a day to Godalming during the period of their bus operations finishing in the village at 5.20 p.m. On a Saturday, they would pick up at 5.45 p.m. to go to the Hippodrome at Aldershot, arriving back in the village at 10 p.m. and then going back to Godalming to pick people up from the "old bugpit" as the picture house in Station Road, run by a Mr Fudger, was popularly known!

The bus business was separate from the garage and to find out how it began we cannot do better than quote the words of the founder himself: *"Sir Edgar Home, late Chairman of the Prudential . . . approached me when I started a carrier's business through Shackleford, Surrey. He asked me if I was interested in running a private bus through Elstead and Shackleford to Godalming daily. I told him I would if I had the money to do it with. Well, we met at his house (now Aldro School) on a Sunday morning, formed a company, five of us, they put up four fifths of the money and I put up one fifth, subject of course to several things. I got a fourteen-seater going and it was quite a success. After twelve months I was called to Sir Edgar's home for a meeting and they thanked me for the way I ran it, and the way I had kept up my payments to buy them out, and so I became the sole proprietor and the bus was then my own. Later on the business grew to five vehicles. Lord and Lady Middleton owned Peperharow Park, adjoining Sir Edgar's property and they all appreciated the Mays for running a private bus service in their district thus keeping out the big bus companies".*

"The big bus companies" unfortunately won in the end, and Mays sold out to the Aldershot and District Traction Company in 1928. May's Motors continued with their haulage business, based in Thursley Road, until the 1990s. In 1936, "many people preferred to cycle to the town because the bus fares were so expensive". Two carriers a day still went to Godalming, and the Farnham carrier still used a pony and cart.

On January 1st 1937, a 30 m.p.h. speed limit was introduced in the village. There were no street lights, and therefore Elstead was not classed as a built up area. A special permit was needed to allow the Council to put up speed limit signs in the village.

Pot or Peat Common (or even Poot Common – as it appears on a map of 1768) was a wilderness of uneven ground, covered with brambles and gorse. It was cleared and drained in 1921 by one Charlie Pitkin. He laid heather branches flat on the ground with earth on top. In 1936, a children's corner with a hockey pitch, football and cricket pitches, and a hard tennis court was made. In 1936, there were two pavilions. One was a wooden hut from the old war-time camp at Witley, placed parallel to Thursley Road, and the other was parallel to Beacon View Road.

In 1921 the council built 12 semi-detached houses, and by 1937 a further 40 council houses were under construction. Two local builders who were much involved in the expansion of the village during this period were Mr Hardy, who has been mentioned before and who was responsible for much of the building along the north side of Milford Road and in Hookley Lane, and Mr S. Allan, who built some of the semi-detached cottages in Thursley Road, between the school and the recreation ground. Hambledon

Pot Common, c.1900.

Rural District Council rules stated that houses were to be six to an acre in the village and two to an acre in the outlying areas, e.g. The Moat. Mains drainage was laid in 1937 – it must have been a welcome improvement in daily life to have the cess-pits emptied once a month free. To have it done more often cost a fairly hefty one pound.

Heath's and Karn's shops sold haberdashery. Both were general shops and had bread rounds in the 1930s. Karn the baker used to be the last house along the Milford Road. The premises were erected in 1891, and in the 1930s, he had two vans delivering daily in Elstead and surrounding villages. In April 1937, bread was 5d. for a two-pound loaf. There was a big rise from 3d. a loaf the previous year! The baker would work from 3 or 4 in the morning until 1p.m. and also from 6-7 p.m. dough making. Bread was still baked on the premises in the 1990s.

Elstead Nurseries were started at Elstead House in the early 1930s by Ernest Ladhams of Southampton. They specialised in herbaceous plants and landscape and rock gardening. A somewhat bizarre footnote to Elstead businesses in the 1930s is supplied by Gammaton Kennels who, we are told, bred Great Danes, some of which were exported to Australia for kangaroo hunting!

On Oct 19th 1790, Daniel Edsell, the younger, received Elstead Forge on the death of his father (Court Rolls of the Manor of Farnham). He had to pay the sum of 8d. for the privilege of inheriting one cottage with a garden and curtilage and "one meadow called

Waremead containing by estimation one acre and a half". Edsell immediately surrendered his claim to the property, and eventually it came into the hands of John Newland, gentleman, of Seale in 1799. John Paine came from Tilford to carry on the trade of blacksmith in Elstead. In 1821 he became the owner of the property, and was followed by his son, William, who left it to his wife. In 1835, William Paine, was given half an acre of land on Thursley Road as compensation for losing his grazing rights on the common after the enclosure. He promptly sold it for £10. William Paine seems to have been a somewhat volatile character. He was apparently a regular poacher and deer "uplifted" from Peperharow Park were hung on hooks in the bedroom of Forge Cottage. On one occasion, when driving hares into nets set across the road at Warren Lodge, Thursley, he and his friend heard the guard's trumpet as the mail coach came along the road. They just managed to dash out in time and gather up their nets, thus escaping detection.

The cottage attached to the Forge had an open fire on the hearth until about 1860. The ashes were collected each morning in a wheelbarrow and wheeled into the kitchen. Once a week the stone floor was swilled down and the mud brushed into a slush hole in the corner of the room, whence a pipe took it to the cess pool. Fires burnt turf and peat. Turf was cut in summer and placed in heaps to dry. It was collected after harvest in a waggon, and taken around the village for delivery to the various houses.

The Forge was probably set up solely for farriery, but later took on a considerable amount of iron work. In 1882, we find them doing such things as "laying colter and screw to plough wheel 2/-", "Altering mowing machine", "Putting spud in handle 6d.", "Mending wire to lamp 3d.", "Two rivets to spud 4d.". There were two forges and four men in the heyday of the Forge to cope with the business. W.H. Bovington, who had been apprenticed to Paine, took over from him, and the business later passed to his son Guy.

G.W. Ellis had his milk round, with the dairy at the corner at West Hill. He obtained milk from Stacey's Farm, which was run by Walter Ellis, his father, thus neatly keeping it all in the family. Stacey's Farm was owned at the turn of the century by Col. Rushbrook who was a considerable landowner in this area of the village. He let it to several tenants before selling it outright to Walter Ellis.

Darkie Ellis would do two journeys a day to Godalming, fetching coal, 5 cwt at a time. It must have been a regular chore for anyone travelling to Godalming to have to get out and open the gates across the road. There was one at Royal Common and two at Shackleford Road.

Weyburn Engineering, later Weyburn Bartel, was the only real factory in the village. It employed about 300 people in 1937, and made lifeboat engines and parts for cars and aeroplanes. During the Second World War, it went over to the making of munitions, and was staffed largely by women workers. In 1931, Weyburn Engineering Company manufactured a device patented by A.R. Pitchers, a knitting firm of Godalming, for making a whole row of cable stitches at once. The name Weyburn has now entirely disappeared, as the premises are now used by a firm called Federal Mogul.

Hop picking over at Puttenham was an annual event until the Second World War. Women would leave the village daily at 7p.m., returning at 5p.m., travelling by May's transport. Carrots would be put on the train at Milford Station for Covent Garden. They were washed and packed at Ellis's Farm, now the British Legion. Life was still largely agricultural, but there was more contact with the outside world. In the 1930s we are told, most of the Godalming tradesmen delivered daily in Elstead.

At Bowler's Stores in Milford Road, it was a regular sight to see an old donkey cart waiting to start the bread round. Mr Terry, the butcher, had a wooden shack where Potter's Delicatessen now is. He kept open until 11 p.m. on a Saturday night. Jack Reffold had a fried fish shop nearby, in Back Lane. There was still no doctor in the village, however, and men would cycle to Milford after work to get a bottle of medicine. Houses in outlying districts, such as Hankley Common, still burnt oil lamps and cooked with wood fires in the 1930s, but the main part of the village had gas and electricity laid on to the houses in 1925.

There must have been a fair amount of poverty in the early years of the twentieth century. Very few people had only one occupation, and Miss Wand, who in 1937 had been doing charity work in the village for at least 30 years, said that when she began many people were in ragged clothes and nearly starving. She always gave food and clothes, never money, and collected from her friends to supply these.

The River Wey had always caused problems with flooding in the low lying areas in its immediate vicinity. Waverley Abbey was flooded on many occasions in the time of the monks. There were regular reports of children not getting through to Elstead School in the late 19th and early 20th centuries because of the floods. In 1935, action was finally taken. The whole course of the river was cleared of weeds, and drainage channels dug to the lower river level. The tributaries were widened and deepened, and a canal was made near Somerset Bridge. A flood path or raised bridge was built across the fields from the river to Polshot Farm. All this activity certainly paid off, because when the next floods came, in 1936-37, they were nothing like as bad as previously. It was felt at the time improvements were carried out that they might help to prevent the flood waters of the Wey from piling up so badly at Guildford as they had done in 1901, and again in 1928. There were, of course, severe floods again in Guildford in 1968, so perhaps this hope was in vain.

A "temporary" bridge was built during the Second World War, beside the existing Elstead Bridge. After the way of these things, it was never taken down, and so became permanent, giving the existing two-way traffic, each lane using a different bridge. Elstead had distinguished visitors during the last war, although maybe not many of the villagers were aware of it. Sir Winston Churchill and General de Gaulle watched a demonstration in a field by Elstead bridge, of a tank-like vehicle, which opened out mechanically to form a bridge.

During the Second World War, huts, including a cinema, were set up on the Green at Westbrook for the army. Youngsters from the village were invited to the cinema from time to time. Westbrook House was the Canadian Officers' Mess, and troops were billeted in Elstead house, The Old Rectory, and elsewhere in the village.

Guinea Common and Cut Mill were ploughed up to grow potatoes, and the RAF had a camp, with tents and an airstrip, on part of Guinea Common. Access to Guinea Common was controlled by a RAF sentry at the top of Hookley Lane.

When the soldiers were short of money they would come into the village wearing four or five coats and sell them off! You could also buy boots, shirts and leather jerkins. The local boys all had a leather jerkin with a maple leaf on the back! Local lads would also forage on the rubbish dumps and find windscreens and headlamps from the soldiers' Harley Davidson motorbikes, and fit them onto their pedal cycles!

There was a prisoner of war camp located in Nissen huts in the grounds of Aldro School, as it is now. Some of the prisoners worked on the land at Woodside Farm, but the Germans and Italians had to be kept apart, or they would fight! Friday night would also see fights on the Village Green between the RAF and the Canadians!

Tanks were based in Peperharow Park, some of which were made of rubber and inflated as decoys.

Lorries were driven through the Moat Pond, using a wiremesh road laid through the water. There was a large ramp on the far side of the pond, and if a lorry broke down in the pond a soldier would go out on a raft, hook a winch rope to the front and drag it out with the winch. Local boys, not surprisingly, loved to get into the back of the lorries prior to them going through the water!

On the Elstead to Shackleford road there was a rodeo known as "Calgary". Genuine cowboys were brought over from Canada for these shows to entertain the troops.

The Home Guard used a hut at the rear of the Village Hall, and also manned a lookout point at the top of the hill behind "Mill Mere", Stacey's Farm Road – Bonfire Hill. May Knott, the village nurse, volunteered one evening to deliver a message from the hut to the lookout point. The short cut was via the cemetery, and as she emerged from the cemetery gates into the road, dressed all in white, she saw a group of Canadian soldiers, returning

Home Guard Sergeant George Chandler with his son, Bob, and daughter, Rosemary

from an evening in the pub, tearing off down the road in the direction of Thursley! Thus are ghost stories born!

Chandlers Garage had three pumps during the war. One was for the sole use of the National Fire Service, whose headquarters were at River House, with fire tenders parked on the Village Green. The second pump was for the army, and the third for private use by coupon holders. George Chandler was restricted to a 15 mile radius of the village with his taxi service.

The two developments which affected the village to the greatest extent during the twentieth century, were undoubtedly those of housing, and social life. We have seen how improvements in transport made possible visits to the Hippodrome at Aldershot, and the Picture Palace at Godalming. Nor was home-grown entertainment lacking. In 1911, the village was entertained by a "Coronation Play", which was held in Rectory Meadows, on June 14th and 17th of that year. The play, which was written by Mr F.A. Lyall, a gentleman staying in the neighbourhood, had the Rev. R.N. Curwen as pageant master. *"There was an audience of close on 500 at the performance . . . the meadow made an admirable stage representing the Village Green. Beyond, the River Wey was flowing peacefully, and was spanned by a rude bridge, over which passed the road to Farnham"*. Various scenes in the history of the village were depicted in passages of somewhat flowery language! One scene, which is supported by an account in the Annals of Waverley Abbey, told how Sir John de Shackleford carried off the Abbey shoemaker. This arrest was a breach of the privileges of the church, as the shoemaker had taken sanctuary in the Abbey. Sir John appeared with his prisoner, but refused to release him when demanded to do so by the Abbot, and was promptly excommunicated for his pains! King Henry III, out hunting from his favourite castle at Guildford, appeared and was appealed to by the Abbot in whose favour he decided. This scene, we are told, "gave opportunities for really fine acting, as the Abbot, the Rev. R.N. Curwen performed with dramatic intensity and histrionic skill".

If they could not quite rival the impact of this special event, there were many societies establishing themselves in the village providing social contacts of a more regular kind. The Scouts were affiliated to the Farnham Association by 1917. Elstead Football Club was registered with the Surrey Football Association. Weyburn ran their own football team for a time.

Elstead Football Club was formed in 1911, by Mr G. Carter, a local schoolmaster, and Guy Bovington, the village blacksmith. They played all in white at Weyfield (Weyburn). Activities were suspended during the First World War, and resumed again in 1921, this time as the Elstead Village Hall Football Club, playing on a ground which at that time belonged to Col. Cornwall, at Burford Lodge, and wearing blue shirts and white shorts. Two "Smoking Concerts" were held in 1921-22 to raise funds for the club. One raised 9s. and the other, the following March, a further 7s. In the 1924-25 season Elstead won promotion to Division 1 of the Farnham and District League. This success led to the creation of a new pitch at the Thursley Road Recreation Ground. Nearly 800 loads of soil were carted to the ground by volunteers, but the committee were severely reprimanded by Hambledon RDC for removing too much soil from the roadside! In 1952, the club joined the Guildford and District League, the most successful period in their history being from 1952 to 1964 when they were league champions on three occasions. The club was elected to the Surrey Intermediate League after 1964, where they remain to this day, having been league champions in the mid 1990s.

We have seen that the schoolboys' cricket club started in 1894, was a success, and there were already adult matches with neighbouring villages, like the one with Thursley in 1890. The season in those days began later, and finished earlier than now, as the majority of the teams were not available for cricket at harvest time. The L'Anson Cup Competition was born at the first annual dinner of the Grayshott Cricket Club at the "Fox and Pelican", in November 1900. The cup was donated by Edward Blakeway L'Anson, a vice-president of the Grayshott Club. In 1922, the Miller Cup was competed for by second elevens and junior clubs. In 1949, Elstead entered both the Miller and L'Anson Cup competitions for the first time. A long and successful playing tradition, coupled with the good wickets on the recreation ground, has resulted in a club which thrives to this day.

The Scouts originally met in a building at the rear of Elstead Mill. They then had their own hut in the grounds of Sandford Farm. Finally, they had a hut on the common between the top of Red House Lane and Gunners Cottages, which has now been demolished.

A photograph of the Elstead Village Band, taken in 1921, shows a proud group, instruments gleaming, and most of them in uniform. Jack Warner was in charge of the band, and another Jack, Jack Bond, had a Minstrel Troupe, which must have been in regular demand for village entertainments. There were no less than three resident bands in the village at one stage, the Brass Band, the Scouts Band and the Fife Band. In the 1950s, Reg Tracy formed a small dance band, and in 1956, a skiffle group was formed – the Delta Skiffle Group, which would play on a Friday evening in the village hall. There was also a weekly film show in the village hall, given by a mobile unit, which visited the villages regularly.

Elstead Village Band, 1921.

Elstead must have catered for most tastes in leisure pursuits in the years before and after the Second World War. There was a cycle speedway track off Thursley Road, where the local club, "The Vampires" met regularly.

The origins of the present Garden Club are to be found in the dark days of the Second World War when growing your own food became more of a necessity than a hobby. In 1943 the Government was seriously concerned to increase food production. To further this aim, Horticultural Advisers were appointed in all districts. Two of them for this area were the late Mr Ernest Ladhams of the Nurseries, and Captain Bonnet. Mr Ladhams became the Garden Club's first president, with Captain Bonnet as chairman. Mrs Violet Gordon, the mother-in-law of the present president, encouraged the club's early years.

Recent years have seen a continued expansion in the range of clubs and societies, with the formation of a very successful tennis club, and PETS – The Players of Elstead Theatrical Society. There was a previous amateur dramatic group in the village in the 1950s, the Cygnets.

Gas was originally supplied to the village by the Aldershot Gas Company, and electricity by overhead cables from the grid system. Not until the 1970s were the cables around the Green put underground. In the mid-1960s, when Elstead acquired street lighting, there was an end to the battle, which had split opinion in the village for nearly 30 years, over whether it was desirable. Coal in the 1930s varied in price from 2s.6d in the winter to 2s.2d in the summer per cwt. Prices were much cheaper from Godalming coal merchants than those in Farnham, as the Godalming merchants were greater in number, and had more competition in selling their coal. Coal was 2s.2d per cwt from Godalming coal merchants, but as much as 2s.10d from those in Farnham.

We have seen that there was a considerable expansion of house building in the village in the 1930s and later, and it is this increase in physical size which did most to form the character of the Elstead we know today. The rateable value in 1936 was £5.18s.10d. per head of the population, less than half that of neighbouring villages such as Busbridge and Tilford.

The building development was, to a large extent, under the control of local people. We have already met the Hardys and their development in Hookley Lane/Milford Road. The Warners, parents of Mr Hardy's wife, lived at Guinea Cottage which is in the parish of Peperharow. The house has largely been lived in by Elstead people, however, and in itself provides a good example of the continuity and interaction of many local families. One and Two Pond Cottages are on Royal Common, close to Guinea Cottage, but they seem to be considerably older. When they were being altered and modernised in 1963, coins of Queen Anne's reign (1702-1714) were found under the floor. The fireplaces would also appear to date from this period, as do some bricked up windows which suggest an eighteenth century existence for the house, and a possible urge to escape the window tax of that period. The cottages were at one time lived in by the gamekeepers on Lord and Lady Midleton's estate at Peperharow. Lady Midleton sold them to Mr Baker at Oxenford Grange, from whom they passed to Dr and Mrs Lascelles in 1962.

The Present Spar Shop, c.1920.

There was once a grocers and general store where Spar and the former chemist now are. The shop sold drapery, bread, groceries and dry goods. The chemist appeared in approximately 1965. Next door, was the Post Office, opened in 1952 by Guy Bovington, when Mrs Martin finally closed the Post Office at "Peacehaven". The chemist moved to Milford Road in 2000, to the site of the former Karn's Bakers.

In 1870, the postman would walk from Godalming, deliver letters in Eashing on the way, and still arrive in Elstead at around 8 a.m! There were two deliveries of post a day in the 1930s, four collections Monday to Friday, three on Saturday, and one on Sunday.

Mellersh's Bank, the property of a well-known local family who have given their name to several places in and around Godalming, was taken over in the 1890s by the Capital and Counties Bank. They, in their turn, succumbed to the power of the bigger organisations and sold out to Lloyd's Bank in the late 1920s. So Lloyds it was who opened up in Elstead. From 1932 onwards, a man would come over once a week from Godalming, on a Friday, and use the back room of Mr Tracy senior, at Greenview, now "Overgreen" as a bank. In 1935, the bank moved to a small building in between Chandlers Garage and Tracy's. Lloyds closed their branch, to much local distress at the turn of the twenty-first century, another small nail in the coffin of village life.

The firm of A.J. Tracy and particularly "Reg" as he is still remembered by many villagers, have been so much bound up with the life of the village in the twentieth century, that it is invidious to mention Elstead without referring to them. Parish councillor, choir master, church organist, organiser of the annual gala, district councillor, founder of the youth club, there was hardly a project connected with Elstead that Reg Tracy was not associated with.

Milford Road, c. 1910.

Back Lane is an interesting little thoroughfare; there are few really old houses, except for Ingleside Cottage which may originally have been a toll house, but Torch Cottage is interesting on account of its name. Mr A. Playfoot lives there, and he changed the name from Pledge Cottage to commemorate the fact that he carried the torch in the Olympic Games of 1948. Laureldene was formerly occupied by the Warner family, already mentioned in connection with Guinea Cottage, and is an illustration of how families tended to move around the village, choosing houses to coincide with their needs at particular periods of their lives. The older houses in Back Lane face towards the lane, not Milford Road, perhaps suggesting that Back Lane may have been the original thoroughfare.

A large barn near the Star Inn was demolished when the roadway was altered to make the Springfield Estate. The stabling at Ham Farm has been altered to make four cottages, and the rest of the land has five modern bungalows, set back from Milford Road by their own private concrete drive, upon it. Burford Lea has ten modern bungalows arranged along a private drive – the old driveway to Burford Lodge. The stables of the Lodge are now converted into a house, and the house itself is split into four.

May Cottages in Milford Road were built by the Cornwall family from Burford Lodge for their staff. The Tuck Shop was opened in 1959 by Mr Harold Andrews when it moved from its previous site, in a wooden shop next to the URC Church. The bakery was opened on the site of the present chemist in 1971 but, as we have seen, bread was baked and sold before this by Aubrey Karn in the Karn's grocery shop nearby. Before the First World War a cycle repair shop was run on the site by Mr Alan Pullen. Around 1935, Karns opened a

Elstead before the Springfield and Springhill development.

69

butcher's shop in a small wooden hut on the site. Where the antiques shop now is was a bakehouse and shop owned and run by the Bedford Bowler family, until Karns took it over in 1905, and closed it early in the 1970s.

The Tuck Shop became two new shops for the Millennium. After a very brief period of existence as a butcher and a baker, they are now, depressingly, standing empty.

Avenue House, demolished in the 1960s, had a clothes shop attached to it, kept by Mrs Sally Bowler. In front of the house and parallel to the road, two shops were erected, made from First World War huts from the Canadian camp at Witley. In the Milford end shop Mr Terry had a confectionery business which was later rented by Mr Baker and then by Mr Andrews, before he moved to the final site of the Tuck Shop in 1959. A Mr Bowles rented the Star end shop as a greengrocers. After a fire, and when the Andrews moved, the two wooden shops were demolished, and two modern shops with flats above were built in the 1960s. The end nearest the Star was Pride's Fruiterers and Florist, later the Delicatessen, and No 1 Park View Road was Holroyd's Hardware until it moved to the other end of Avenue Row, then to the Green, finally becoming the doctor's surgery. No 1 then became the fish and chip shop.

Pilgrims was formerly four retirement cottages, built for nursing matrons by A.J. Tracey in 1907 for Mrs Holford of Elstead Lodge, in memory of her father, Mr Pilgrim, and called Pilgrim's Rest. It has now been altered into two semi-detached houses.

The original Tuck Shop.

Withey Bridge, in Farnham Road, started life as Sunny Mount, when it was built in 1901. It was built for a representative of a well-known local name, Mr T. Chalcraft. He married Miss Nellie Watteridge, she who gave the interesting and marathon lectures in the United Reformed Church, and he was a Deacon of the Chapel from 1924. He helped Mr Bovington at the Forge, and was also a postman for a good part of his life.

The meadow opposite the Mill has several interesting features. It has already been mentioned that strip farming survived here until the early 1930s and this was also the site of the flood path, leading across the fields to Polshot Farm. There was only one serious flood since the river and its tributaries were cleared and deepened in the early 1930s, in the early 1970s, that is until the floods of 2000.

The Mill closed as a working mill around 1881, and from 1913 to 1948 the 150-year-old mill wheel was used to generate electricity for the house. In 1963, the roof was rebuilt, and Mr Court-Treat had the water channel made near the road, for the keeping of trout. The property was bought in 1980 by Mr David Riley, who had it completely renovated, got the mill wheel working again and opened it as a restaurant. It has now been sold to a restaurant chain.

Further along the Farnham Road, there are low-lying fields on the left, stretching back to join on to the land owned by the Mill. This was purchased and made into a nature reserve in 1980-81 by the Surrey Trust for Nature Conservation. It consists of 58 acres of meadow and alder woodland where bog beam and marsh cinquefoil grow together – a unique feature. There are 150 different species of plant life. Rabbit, roe deer, fox and badger are all familiar sights.

"Foxhills" on the other side of the road from The Donkey, and further towards Elstead, was the home of Sir Alexander and Lady Anderson who came there in 1938, and altered the house, putting in the large bow window looking towards Elstead. Three Barrows Place, with an obvious clue to earlier remains on the site, was the home of the Rev. Cyril Cresswell, the Queen's Chaplain, and his wife. He died in 1974 and the house is now called Almina Heights.

Fulbrook House was one of the earlier works of Lutyens, many of whose buildings are to be found in this part of Surrey. It was built for Mrs Streatfield, mother of Mrs Violet Gordon.

The Square is a group of cottages situated where the Green and Thursley Road join. This was very much Bowler territory. Two cottages, situated right on the corner of Hope Street and Thursley Road, were pulled down in the late 1950s. The two Victorian/Edwardian cottages on the left of the Square were built by Mr Harry Bowler. From the Farnham Road end, running alongside Hope Street, there was a barn-like structure divided into coal-houses and w.c's for all the houses. It has now been pulled down and altered to form car-ports. Mrs Lamb, nee Bowler, went from her father's grocery store to live at No. 1 the Square after her marriage in 1917 and stayed there until she died, in 1975. Here we have yet another instance which seems to deny the change of twentieth-century life in the village. Mrs Lamb's husband, Jack Lamb, did shoe making in a wooden shop in the garden, and was band master of the Elstead Brass Band. He also sold fireworks when they became available again after the War, running a club where money for them could be paid in throughout the year.

The four houses which used to be in Cedar Mount, leading off Hope Street and running behind the Golden Fleece and Bridge House, have now become two and are lived in by the Tracy family. It was in one of these cottages in the section of road joining Cedar Road and Hope Street that Bill Stilwell lived. Bill was a mole catcher, and gardener to Lloyd George at Churt. The old Recreation Ground was originally Glebe Land but was bought from the Church Commissioners by Mr Dick May, whose career we have already considered, to build a house – Glebe Cottage – for his family and to house his growing business.

Elstead in the 1930s was known as a holiday resort, with many local residents letting rooms in the summer, and week-end cottages being much in evidence.

The old village hall was given to the village by Mr Pilgrim, of Elstead Lodge, and a plaque to that effect hung in the entrance hall. It was enlarged by the addition of a billiard room

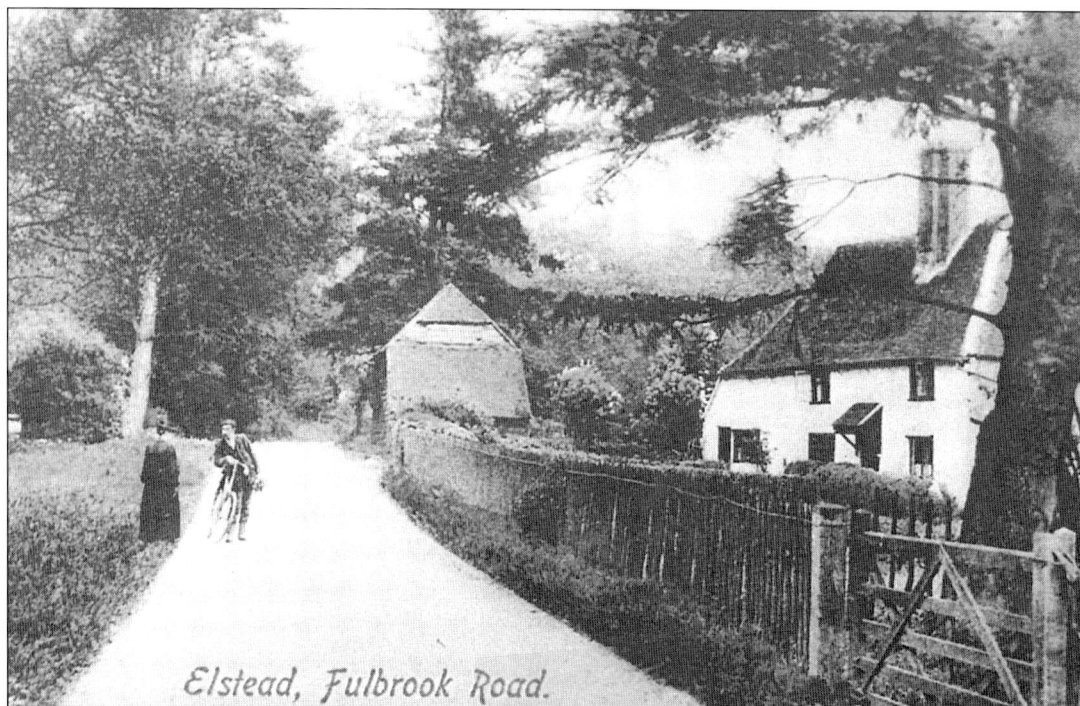

Fulbrook Road, c. 1910.

72

and a house at the back for a caretaker. During the night of March 24th, 1972 there was a disastrous fire and the whole building burnt down. It is one of the many examples of the inspiration of Reg Tracy in village affairs that money was collected to pay for rebuilding and a new hall opened on May 2nd 1975. The old telephone exchange finally abandoned by the Post Office in 1981 was converted and opened as a Youth Centre, again with Reg Tracy's help.

The Gables originally had a shop at the end nearest to the church. A Mr Atkins had a general store there and also ran one of the several carriers' businesses – from Elstead to Farnham. It became a sweet shop, an electrical shop, and is now a private house again.

The Restaurant was the Co-op Stores from the 1930s until the late 1960s and the present Poodle Parlour was a hairdresser's shop in 1935. What is now No. 1 Allendale Cottages was originally a sweet shop, kept by a Mrs Voice. Mr Allen, who lived in the White House, Thursley Road, then called Hill House, has already figured in our story. He was the developer whose special concern this little area of the village was. He had Allendale Cottages, a block of six, built in 1897, and also several houses in Moors Lane, next door.

Briants Stores was built in 1928, as a house for Bill Novell. The front room was later converted into a shop, selling ice cream, sweets and newspapers. Mr Novell delivered the newspapers using a motorcycle and sidecar, having sorted them in the timber section of

Elstead Village Hall, 1911.

the Woolpack and, later, in the Village Hall. He also repaired bicycles in a shed behind the shop.

The Poodle Parlour in Thursley Road was originally a cycle shop and was later owned by Michael Foley, gent's hairdresser. The shop next door was originally a fish shop, but Mr Pride senior converted it into a tea shop during the war. The sticky currant buns costing one penny each were a favourite with local children. Mr Pride's sons, Norman and Neville, later had the shop for general groceries and wet fish. Its latest incarnation was as Coopers, the solicitors, which closed in 2000.

We have already traced much of the history of Little Barn in Ash Lane, and seen that it was tied up with that of Domford, which the Legg family held as tenants of the Bishop of Winchester. The Leggs held Domford itself right up until 1963. Little Barn, however, had passed out of the family hands a long while before. In 1859, Henry Moorey, gardener, was a tenant of the Bishop of Winchester, and in 1923 Ernest Henry Moorey, a baker, bought it from the Ecclesiastical Commissioners. The name Little Barn does not appear until 1946 when it was bought by a Mrs McAllister. Before that it was known as Durnford in 1859, Durnsford in 1922, and Dunsfold in 1936, when it was extended and altered by William Holmes, a carpenter.

Myrtle Cottage was also owned at one time by the Leggs of Domford. They sold it to S. Pride in 1957. The Leggs have long Elstead credentials. They owned The Shack, in Thursley Road, which seems to have been the collective name for three more of the wooden bungalows from the Canadian camp. They were demolished in the 1970s and three modern bungalows built in their place. Mr Jack Legg had a stutter and seems to have been a well-known local character – he was nicknamed "Mutton Leg". He was a "Lengthsman", i.e. responsible for the maintenance of a certain length of road. His length ran right through the village.

At first the headmaster of the village school lived in the house provided, but by 1931 he had moved to Red House Lane and there was a caretaker in the house attached to the school. The old National School was demolished in 1976, and Guardian Court began building on the site. It is now a group of flats for the aged, which houses 38 elderly people with a warden, and was opened in 1978. The new school, Elstead Church of England First School, was opened in 1969, and a swimming pool was added in 1972.

In 1936, we read a fairly gloomy report that "there is not a good farm in Elstead. Fields that formerly yielded rich harvests of corn, hops and carrots are now rough pastures, fast returning to the wild state". Notwithstanding this, Mr W. Trussler seems to have had a fairly lively career. He farmed at "The Moors" and "Domford", both on the Thursley Road, and he was also licensee of both the Star and the Woolpack at different times. When he was at the Star he also ran a building business and was the local undertaker. Truly a "Jack of all trades". He built Beacon View Cottage as his home in about 1922. His son,

Mr A. Trussler who was born at the Star in 1907, followed his father into the building trade. He built Redcot in Beacon View Road in 1928.

Sandford Farm was owned around 1935 by a dentist, Dr Lang. Mrs Elliott of Sandford Farm had a sweetshop, and later her son, Sammy Elliott, ran a cycle repair shop and petrol pump there. Sandford House, now demolished, with a modern bungalow built on the site, was built as a smallholding by Mr John Pearce. The Pearce's have already been mentioned as having almost proprietary rights over this area of the village, and John Pearce and his wife owned and farmed all the land from Moors Lane to Copse Edge. The ownership then passed to their daughter, who became Mrs Sid Ellis, and her husband. A watercress bed was farmed, well off the highway.

Sandford Farm Cycle Shop and Petrol Pump.

Charlie Legg, another of the Legg family, began life as a drover at Guildford cattle market. By 1956, he was postman, and had inherited Domford from George Legg. He kept his two donkeys on part of the Domford land, and sold off other parts for building.

In the twentieth century, the Moat became very popular as a recreational area. The land around the Moat was formerly owned by Col. Whitbread, and was bought in 1978 by the Nature Conservancy Council for a reserve for wildlife and called the Thursley National Nature Reserve. It continued to be managed by the Surrey Trust for Nature Conservation, who had done so for the previous owner. In June 1976, in a summer of drought, there was a terrible fire which burned for several days on the common, and much of the wild life

The Moat, 1930s.

was destroyed. The area of common land stretching back towards Woolfords Lane was, at the turn of the century, part of the Cosford Estate. The War Department bought much of this from the Estate when the latter was sold.

Woolfords Farm was originally farmed by Mr Jack Shrubb, who was also a Common Keeper. Clem Reed was his successor, and he was a well-known figure in the village, delivering milk with his horse and cart. The major suppliers of milk, however, were still the Ellis's at Stacey's Farm. The farm usually had about twenty cows, and three or four heifers. Bull calves were fattened for a week, or longer if milk was plentiful, and then taken to market. Horses were used for general farm work and, until the 1930s, a pony was kept to do the milk delivery. A motor van was then acquired. Crops grown were mainly for cattle food: mangolds, swedes, turnips, kale, rye, clover and oats. Wheat was also grown, and potatoes, carrots and parsnips for the produce market. At first, the farm was able to supply the 30 gallons of milk delivered daily on the milk round. When the amount rose to 50 gallons, however, extra milk had to be brought in from other farms. In 1937, Karns at Somerset Farm were supplying Ellis's with 30 gallons of milk a day, and Perretts at Thundry Farm, with 20 gallons a day, once Stacey's Farm itself had been sold to a builder.

"Golden Acres", in Woolfords Lane, was once a residential hotel and, after the war, a country club. There was a sanitorium near Golden Acres and the building was later occupied by the Ragless family. It burnt down one day, luckily while the family were out.

There was a slight delay before the fire tender could be got to the scene from its base on the Village Green – weeds had to be removed from the door in front of the shed before it could be opened!

Volunteer with the fire appliance, c. 1910.

Up to and immediately after the First World War Red House Lane was merely a footpath as far as Red House Farm. The land was owned by Col. Rushbrook and Mr Dick May approached him about the infant branch of the British Legion which he had started and which, after meeting in various cottages, had now grown in numbers to the extent where they wanted a permanent home. Col. Rushbrook gave them the piece of land where the Roman Catholic Church later stood. Mr May managed to get an old army hut from Bramshott and put it up on the land. The footpath grew to a cart track and became known as Legion Lane. When Mr Billmeir gave the Legion Staceys Farm for their headquarters, the old hut was sold to the Roman Catholics, and the lane became known as Red House Lane. In 1965 Elstead Parish Council discussed the making up of Ham Lane, Red House Lane and Beacon View Road, requiring payments in proportion from the houses then built along those lanes. Red House Lane is the only one entirely made up to date. The Catholic

Church of Our Lady of the Assumption was built in 1969, in place of the old British Legion hut which the church had acquired in 1949. Previous to that, the Roman Catholics had worshipped in an old granary, converted to a chapel by Col. Fitzgerald at Royal Farm, the granary being pulled down in 1953. There is now no Roman Catholic Church building in the village, the nearest being at Milford.

Westbrook House, after being used by the army during the Second World War, was bought by Mr Jack Billmeir in 1946. He founded the Stanhope Shipping Company and had the nickname "Potato Jack" as he had made his money shipping potatoes during the Spanish Civil War. After his sudden death, in 1962, his widow and brother continued to manage the estate. The refurbishing of St James's Church in 1970, when the choir and organ console were moved to the south aisle, and the chancel refurbished and carpeted, was dedicated to the memory of Mr Billmeir. The Billmeir Trust has continued to benefit the village in a number of ways since the death of Mr Billmeir's brother Eric.

So life in Elstead during the twentieth century has seen a significant growth in the area of the village, with the in-filling of all the land along the roads leading through the village, and the development along roads like Ham Lane and Red House Lane, which were formerly footpaths. New estates at Springfield and Hazelwood have added considerably to the population of the village. Transport has improved and so has the quality of life for

Changes continue in Elstead. This is Hillbrow Motors on the May's Motors site. The garage and the house have now (2001) been swept away for new housing.

78

most of the inhabitants. The village retains a vigorous local identity, although it is inevitable with such a large influx of population that the majority no longer work in the direct neighbourhood. The thriving local societies have already been mentioned, as has the solid core of local population with several generation roots in the area. It is this quality of permanence, underlying the shifts and changes of modern development, which perhaps makes Elstead that little bit special and ensures that in a sense Elstead then will be carried on into Elstead now, tomorrow, and all the years to come, in the best tradition of English village life.

An event unique to Elstead is the Paper Boat Race. Recently revived after a break, it is held annually at the Moat. Boats are large enough for passengers and some stay afloat for a considerable time!

POSTSCRIPT

This is a re-working of my original outline sketch of the history of Elstead, first produced over fifteen years ago under the title "Yesterday in Elstead" and now, except for the Internet version, out of print. I am very conscious of the fact that there is always more to learn about Elstead and no doubt in a few years there will be ample scope for yet another edition.

I would like to record my sincere thanks to Mrs Carol May, without whose help this book would never have seen the light of day, also to Mr Clive Warren, for his help and information, and permission to use his picture collection. Mrs Prue Bardelli and Mrs May Deaville started me on this road over fifteen years ago, and I would like to repeat my thanks to them and to all those who then and since have supplied me with information. I hope they will pardon my deficiencies and enjoy reading about Elstead Then and Now. My thanks also go to Mr Alan Collis who laboured to transfer my text to the Internet.

A special thank you to Mr Richard Holmes and Mr "Billy" Bennett for their lovely illustrations for the front and back covers respectively. I was particularly delighted that two local artists felt they would like to be involved with the production.

We are indebted to the Francis Frith Collection, Salisbury, Wiltshire SP3 5QP, www.francisfrith.co.uk for permission to reproduce the illustration of Elstead Village Hall, and to the Surrey Archaeological Society for permission to reproduce the maps, the cover from the Parish Magazine, and the two pictures of Elstead Church, by Petrie and Saunders.

For those who are interested, there follows a list of the main sources I have consulted:

Baker, John L. A Picture of Surrey. Robert Hale, 1980.

Cleal, Edward. Congregationalism in Surrey. James Clark, 1908.

Connell, John. The End of Tradition? Country Life in Central Surrey. Routledge, 1978.

Coronation Play held in Rectory Meadows Elstead on June 14th and 17th 1911, together with a cutting from the Surrey Times describing the same.

Domestic Buildings Research Group. Report on Domford, Thursley Road, Elstead. Surrey Record Office.

Dugmore, Ruth. Puttenham Under the Hog's Back. Phillimore, 1972.

Elstead Census Returns.

    Churchwarden's Accounts.

    Parish Magazines 1890-91.

    Parish Registers.

Farnham – Court Rolls of the Manor.

Gover, J.E.B. Place Names of Surrey. C.U.P., 1934.

Manning, O. and Bray, W. History of Surrey, 3 vols. John White, 1804-1814.

Medcalf, Olive. Elstead – thesis completed for a teacher training course 1936.

Notes on the History of Oxenford Typescript.

Parker, Eric. Highways and Byways in Surrey. Macmillan, 1923.

Rent Rolls of the Bishop of Winchester.

Robo, E. Medieval Farnham. Langham, 1939.

Surrey Advertiser, May 6th 1983. Elstead Mill by John Baker.

Surrey Archaeological Collections, vol. 6, 1870. Elstead and its Church, pp.192-202.

Surrey Record Society.   Hearth Tax Returns.

                    Quarter Sessions Records.

                    Wills.

Surrey Times, June 3rd 1845. The Laying of the Foundation Stone of the New Chapel at Elstead.

Victoria County History of Surrey, edited by H.E. Malden, 4 vols. Constable, 1912.